The Woodwright's Companion

THE
WOOD WRIGHT'S
COMPANION

Exploring Traditional Woodcraft

Roy Underhill

THE UNIVERSITY OF NORTH CAROLINA PRESS

CHAPEL HILL AND LONDON

First printing, April 1983
Second printing, September 1984
Third printing, November 1985

Library of Congress Cataloging in Publication Data

Underhill, Roy.
The woodwright's companion.

Bibliography: p.
Includes index.
1. Woodwork.   2. Woodworking tools.   I. Title.
TT180.U467   1983   684′.082   82-20077
ISBN 0-8078-1540-3
ISBN 0-8078-4095-5 (pbk.)

Photo credits:
Scottie Austin p. 19(a); Claire Mehalick p. 30(b); Geary Morton pp. 1, 4.
All others by R.E.U.

To Jane.
Broadway's loss is
our gain.

Contents

Thanks

I am deeply grateful for the generous assistance given me by the staff of the Colonial Williamsburg Foundation. The director of the Department of Historic Trades, Earl L. Soles, Jr., my stalwart crew, Mark Berninghausen, Bill Weldon, Garland Wood, William Alexander, and Doug Austin, my colleagues Peter Ross, George Wilson, Wallace Gusler, Jay Gaynor, George Pettengell, Kerry Shackelford, Robin Phillips, Dan Stebbins, Lew LeCompte, Edward Chappell, Jim Waite, Paul Buchanan, Dave Salisbury, Gary Brumfield, George Suiter, Kelly Blanton, Vanessa Patrick, Roy Black, and Raymond Townsend, and the staffs of the Cabinet Shop and the Gunsmith Shop have all been a tremendous help, and I thank you all.

Many friends have helped by the loan of tools to show and couches to sleep on. To Dr. William McClendon, Robert M. Leary, Fred and Margaret Bair, Martha Blee, Pam and Snuffy Smith, Maggie the dog, Tom and Jean Wescott, Donna Hayes, Sid Rancer, and Linwood and Sue Ann go my heartfelt thanks.

Thanks also to professors J. Robert Butler and Fred M. White for technical and research assistance and to Jamestowne Festival Park and Old Salem, Incorporated, for location work.

The staff of the University of North Carolina Center for Public Television, especially Geary Morton, director, Bobby Royster, executive producer, and Alvin Hall, publicist, deserves great credit for its splendid work on the Public Broadcasting System series "The Woodwright's Shop."

Thanks again to the folks at the University of North Carolina Press, especially David Perry, Johanna Grimes, Anne Dodd, and Guinn Batten, for their work on the book. Thanks for lunch, too.

Introduction

We are creators and teachers. The confidence of humankind is based not on superior strength or speed but on our abilities to shape the materials of our environment and to communicate our experiences.

This book is the second that I have prepared to teach traditional American woodcraft. The first volume, "The Woodwright's Shop," followed the progression that I have used in my workshop classes, "how to start with a tree and an axe and make one thing after another until you have a house and everything in it." This book follows a similar path, beginning with tools and trees and finishing with the house—but making a lot of side trips on the way.

At its most basic level, this book is a guide to the making of the items described here. Beyond that, though, these processes and products are keys to a deeper perception of the ways man relates to the material world.

As much as such things can be spoken of, I explore some of these patterns in the text of this book. But true knowing can come only as you work with the wood.

With each swing of the axe, each joining of the wood, you build and preserve within you the living memory of this timeless trade.

The satisfaction that you gain is well deserved.

FINDING

Everythings got a moral if only you can find it.

Lewis Carroll, *Alice's Adventures in Wonderland* (1865)

Scrap steel is carefully weighed before sale.

In the old shop where I worked about fifteen years ago, an old fellow came in every week to sharpen the handsaws. He made his living doing this, and we looked forward to seeing him set up his sharpening vise in a corner of the shop. He was a devoutly religious man, or at least he seemed to be, because he was always quiet until he overheard a bit of profanity escape the lips of one of the workers. With that he would launch into a diatribe on how each word had nailed another spike into the offender's scaffold of eternal damnation. Occasionally, someone would feign a hammer blow to his thumb and let fly with a choice blasphemy to set him off, but for the most part we left him alone with his work.

After I had been working there for about a year, the shop got a new foreman. He looked at this man in the corner with jealousy. It was not the few dollars the old man charged for his work that bothered him, but the fact that the old fellow knew how to sharpen saws and he didn't. The new foreman couldn't stand this and went out and bought a set of saw-sharpening tools. Every week when the old man came in, the new foreman would set up some pretense of woodwork in the vise across the bench from him and surreptitiously attempt to learn the secrets of his trade. The old man knew what was going on, of course, and constantly tried to reposition himself to cover his work. The foreman was persistent, though, and as the weeks wore on, the old man grew increasingly resentful of this transparent act of thievery.

One day when the foreman was a few minutes into his spying he was abruptly called away to accept delivery of a new load of lumber. As soon as the door closed behind him, the old man called for all the rest of us in the shop to come over. In five minutes he explained with a vengeance all there was to know about

saw sharpening. Just as he was finishing, we saw the foreman coming up the path. The old man saw him too, gathered up his tools, and threw them in his satchel. Storming out toward the door he stopped, turned to us, pointed his finger at each of us in turn, and said, "Any one of you that shows that G-- damned son of a bitch how to sharpen a saw goes straight to hell!"

He never came back and we never did.

The commonplace items and ideas of the past become scarce as their usefulness is diminished and they are replaced by the new. As time passes, they may become desirable again either because interest in former values revives or because their increasing scarcity gives them worth in a somewhat mercenary sense. The two are not incompatible.

The problem, or rather the opportunity, is that the things you need may well be in the hands of other people. They are often willing to part with or share what they possess if given something of value in return—and a chance to make something on the deal. He gets your twelve dollars and you get his old jack plane. Both parties feel better off than they were before the transaction. An ice storm brings down trees in your neighborhood; you clean up the mess in exchange for the wood. Everyone is happy. The old fellow down the lane shares with you his wisdom (or lack of it) in exchange for a sympathetic ear.

These are the obvious ways and the most fruitful. Making the rounds of antique dealers, junk yards, and auction houses, you get to know the people and how to deal with them. You learn how to get the discount price at antique shops. You overcome "bidding fever" at auctions (events which still leave me a nervous wreck). You spot big trees and come running when you hear a power saw in the neighborhood. You talk to the people

who remember, who know. You study what they have made. It's like hunting; you must start doing it and keep doing it until opportunity meets preparation with increasing frequency.

Of course it's not always easy or straightforward. We are human, after all. In my younger days, having just overcome my shyness about haggling over prices, I fancied myself a pretty shrewd customer. An old country scrap dealer with whom I'd had few dealings had a set of hollow augers that I wanted. He allowed as how he didn't want to sell them because he might want to make something with them someday.

I argued and cajoled sporadically as we looked about the yard at other stuff, but he was obstinate. There was another man present, one with whom he had more regular dealings, who kept telling me that I was wasting my time trying to get this fellow to change his mind. Feeling full of myself, though, I insisted that we go back to look at the augers and embarked on a lengthy discourse aimed at convincing him to sell the darn things to me. I knew he wasn't going to use them, but he remained unmoved throughout.

Finally I threw up my hands and said, "I give up. You're just too tough for me." With that he put them in my hands and said, "Twelve bucks for the three of them." Maintaining his dominance over the situation was much more important to him than the money. We've been doing business ever since.

Sometimes people just don't want to sell, and you just have to accept that. One year a huge California redwood that had been planted as an ornamental a hundred years before on one of the old estates across the river went down in a storm. I wanted it bad, but the old couple who lived there didn't know me and gave it instead to their old handyman, who proceeded to cut it up into firewood lengths. I spoke to him and tried to convince him that there was better wood to burn than redwood and that I would gladly supply an equal volume of hickory in exchange. Knowing that I wanted it, though, that I might get more use out of the tree than he would, made him want it just that much more. He kept it and burned it. It was his. You meet these people now and then.

You need good tools, not necessarily old ones. Before I go on about what to look for in buying old tools, I must say a bit about the ethics of the trade—not the ethics of buying and selling but of using up a nonrenewable resource. Interest in the history of the working man is increasing, and his tools constitute some of the most important records of that history. We are the guardians of this information; when you buy and use old tools you hold a key to the past in your hands. Abuse can destroy this key, and the information that it holds can be lost forever. We all have the responsibility to determine, either by checking with an expert or becoming experts ourselves, just how rare a key we hold. We all come out ahead when we trade a rare plane to a collection in exchange for more common planes to use.

Metal

Early edge tools were often made of two different sorts of metal. The body of the tool was wrought iron for toughness and strength. Wrought iron, though, is too soft to hold an edge. To make a hard cutting edge, a layer of tool steel was then forge welded onto the flat (unbeveled) side of the blade. The result was a tough, strong tool that would take and hold a razor edge.

Pitting from corrosion is the great

A pile of defective axes discovered at the scrap yard.

Although severely pitted, this cooper's adze has enough steel left to be useful.

enemy of these tools. If an edge tool has been severely pocked by corrosion on the flat face, you may never be able to get it right again. If the pits are not too deep, you may be able to regrind the flat below their depth. Sometimes the pits go all the way through the steel, in which case you have a collector's item.

Another thing to watch for is a tool that in the normal course of sharpening has been ground beyond the length of the applied steel. You can usually see this, but if you are in doubt, you can pick lightly at the metal with the corner of a file. The file should skate off hardened steel but dig into wrought iron. At the very least you will be able to tell the difference between the two.

Other problems with metal are cracks, missing parts, stripped threads, and pieces that are rusted solid. Don't be too confident about overcoming these difficulties until you have gained some experience. Broken steel can be welded and cast iron brazed, but you had best check out the cost before you decide to buy. Missing parts can be forged or cast, but again you had better investigate what this will run you in time and money. A good machine shop can do wonders, but a special job can take extra time, and time is what they charge for.

Stripped threads are not too hard to deal with, as the hole can often be drilled out and tapped larger and a new screw put in its place. You can try to back out a screw that is broken off in the hole by going through the ritual of soaking it in a rust solvent, such as kerosene or one of the commercial varieties, drilling into the screw, and using a screw extractor. Very small screws will not take extractors well, and you may have to try and knock the screw around by digging into one corner with a small cold chisel and tapping with a hammer.

Heating with a blow torch and rapping with a hammer to loosen the rust are classic procedures that have freed many a joint, but also broken quite a few pieces as well. Go gently, patiently. Soak the tool in solvent for weeks and try it again every now and then.

For general corrosion, you again want to use the gentlest process. Rather than attack it with commercial rust eater and high-speed wire brushes, try boiling the tool in distilled water for five minutes and brushing gently with a fiber brush. You can escalate your attack slowly, but try to

do the least harm that you can to the original surface. Your patience will be rewarded.

Wood

Broken wood repaired with glue is often stronger than the original piece. Look for existing glue lines in old tools before you buy them. An old repair with old glue may not hold up if it is in a critical spot. Once an old glue joint fails, it must be cleaned down to the bare wood before the new glue can be expected to hold.

Powder post beetles are a constant destroyer of old wooden tools. The larvae tunnel inside the wood, eating as they go. When they mature, they exit through the surface, leaving holes to show that they were there. They then mate, lay eggs in a convenient piece of wood, and begin the cycle again. The more exit holes there are on the surface, the more eating has been going on inside.

If you must resurface the bottom of an old plane that shows exit holes, you will likely cut into the powdery tunnels, exposing them on the new surface. Coating the wood with some

I cracked the part of the wheelwright's tenon cutter or hollow auger in the foreground by tapping too hard. The screws are still rusted solid.

Woodworm damage. The rounder plane is badly eaten. The broken wooden screw on top from a clamp was broken when I bought it, but had been glued back by an unscrupulous dealer. The exit hole of the woodworm that caused the damage is visible on top of the first thread on the right half.

sort of finish is the best defense against them. Remember that the exit holes mean that the beetles have left. Whether a new generation is active inside is not easy to tell, but cleaning solvents will usually kill them if they are.

Wood grows beautiful and grimy with use. What you want to do is remove the grime but not the beauty. Abrasives remove both. A good cleaning solvent for wood is what is called "mineral spirits," available at most hardware dealers. Clean the wood with a soft cloth dampened with this solvent; the grime will go, and the beauty will stay.

Wood does need a protective finish after having been cleaned. The traditional finish is linseed oil, rubbed into the wood until it glows. Planes are traditionally soaked in linseed oil by stopping the bottom of the throat with window putty and keeping the space filled with oil until it comes out either end. Current thought, however, is that, like all enjoyable things, linseed oil may have a bad effect. It apparently feeds an enzyme reaction that softens and slowly (very slowly) degrades the wood. The preferred finish now is some sort of microcrystalline wax. Carnauba wax is good and is readily available. The linseed oil is perhaps best used on new things that you have made, not on old things that you are trying to preserve.

Trees

If the trees don't belong to you, they must belong to somebody else. It feels strange to talk about ownership of living things, but that's the way the planet is set up. I must confess that in my younger, wilder days I "liberated" a score of pine tipi poles from a cove on the side of Cheyenne Mountain in Colorado. It was government land, and I rationalized that since the gov-

A walnut tree in the woods will often lead you to an old cabin, or vice-versa.

The patterns are hard to break.

ernment had taken it from the Indians, it really wasn't theirs either. But that sort of thinking leads to trouble—and regret.

I could have gotten the poles honestly. All I would have had to have done was ask. We still have relatively plentiful timber resources. Look and ask and tell people what you're after and soon they will start coming to you when they have something. There are state and federal forestry people to call on. Firewood cutters, farmers, tree doctors, and the like, all have contact with timber that you can use. One good connection is the people in charge of the landscapes of large institutions like universities. When a big shade tree goes down, you want to know about it.

Unless you are already an expert, it's probably best to pass on wood that would involve dropping trees near houses, cars, and power lines. You could end up with some pretty expensive timber. It can also cost you dearly to go nosing around on other people's property looking for trees. Folks don't like that anymore than you would. You had better ask before you go exploring. For the most part, though, once you get the hang of it, you end up with a lot more wood than you know what to do with. Very soon you'll become a source yourself.

Information

The proliferation of information in our society is both a boon and a curse. Just try and find an old fellow who hasn't been given a book about the old days by his grandchildren and now remembers that as the way it was. The particulars of folk culture are in constant danger of being drowned in a sea of nostalgic generalization. Scholars face this problem all the time. In 1929, Henry Mercer, in his seminal work *Ancient Carpenter's Tools*, coined the term *goose wing* to describe a form of Germanic axe. How he would shudder to hear the way in which the adjective has taken its place in the language, as though this were what pre-Mercer German carpenters called such an axe. They would have known it as *die Barte*, a "bearded" axe. In English, goose wing has become the accepted term and is obviously here to stay. Language is always changing, sometimes through evolution and sometimes through creation. We use what language we wish, but it's important to keep track of where it came from.

The closer you can get to the source, the better off you are. It takes more effort to find the old books, to examine the tool marks left on old timbers, to talk to the people who made them, but you and the world are richer for your labors.

Understanding

Knowledge is one thing; understanding is another. Wood responds to the hands of man in somewhat predictable ways. And the response of wood to the steel blade forms patterns in human behavior. We approach the same problem when it appears in a different context with a similar solution. Woodworking involves the constant repetition of these patterns both in tools and design.

For example, throughout this book—and woodworking in general—you will encounter the "stopping cut" (to borrow a carver's term). When you make a slot through a piece of wood by boring a hole at either end and prying out the wood in between, the holes form the stopping cut. When you make a tenon by sawing across the grain and splitting down to it, the saw has made the stopping cut. The down-cutting lips on an auger make the stopping cut prior to the removal of the wood by the rotary chisel of the auger. Another pattern is revealed when you shear wood across the grain. It responds best to a diagonal, skewed attack with the blade. This is true whether you're spindle turning on a lathe or smoothing a tenon with a plane.

It organizes your thought to find these unities. It helps you understand both form and function. When you look at the way an Englishman builds a house, and then see it reflected in his furniture construction, his window sash, his fences and gates, you're on to something. Patterns begin to emerge that tell you about people.

About the best example I have seen of the "cultural tool box" are reconstructions of historic buildings. Like all forms of historic interpretation, they reflect the best knowledge of the time but can seldom escape the aberrations peculiar to the mirror of the present. In some of the mid-twentieth-century reconstructions of seventeenth-century houses, the builders knew that they "wouldn't have used nails back then." But rather than use mortice and tenon joints secured with pegs, they butted the timbers together, bored long diagonal holes, and drove in pegs, essentially toenailing the buildings with dowels. They used pegs as though they were nails because this fit into a system with which they were familiar. These patterns are hard to break and influence our work in ways that we ourselves are often unable to see.

Folklore too is a tapestry of the intuitive and the rational, sense and nonsense. I had often heard the admonition to "never burn a tree that has been hit by lightning in your fireplace. It'll burn your house down." I considered this to be nonsense until I chanced to be hewing a beam from a pine tree that had been hit by lightning. Beneath the bark I found that down one whole side where the tree had been hit the wood was almost solid resin. The tree had produced the resin to protect the scar from attack by insects and fungi. Had I burned this tree in the fireplace, the resin would have caused such a soot buildup in the flue that a tremendous chimney fire could have resulted and might well have burned the house down.

The works of man affect and are affected by his resources. It's a two-way street. The carving on furniture from southern Europe is done in flat, incised relief. In northern Europe the carving is deep and in bold relief. The difference springs not from different aesthetic judgments but from the different forests in which the people worked. The highlands of southern Europe had abundant softwoods, but no hardwoods that could hold up to high relief carving. Northern Europe had copious amounts of hardwood, and the furniture styles reflected the nature of the material. The trees impose their tastes on us.

THE FOREST

When an oak has fallen every man becomes a woodcutter.

Menander (fourth century B.C.)

On the Ohio River there is a site where the Indians built up a sizable village, lived for a few generations, and then suddenly moved on. After a half century or so they returned to reoccupy the site, only to abandon it again after the same length of tenancy. They repeated this pattern of occupation and abandonment in a regular cycle for around a thousand years, leaving archaeologists with scores of layers to pick through and a mystery to ponder.

The key to the mystery, they discovered, was wood. As the population built up, the people had to travel further and further to find firewood and building material. When the situation became intolerable, they left. After the people were gone, the forest could recover, and when it did, the people returned. Use it up and move on was a reasonable way to deal with resources back when there were places to move on to.

Medieval Europe faced the same problem of dwindling resources, but given its greater population density and established cities, moving on was not a practicable solution. In typical fashion, the members of the ruling class responded to this crisis by carving out a big piece of the pie and claiming it as their own. Indeed, the word *forest* originally meant land reserved for the exclusive use of the king and his cronies. It could include open land as well as wooded. A forester was originally the man who guarded the forest from encroaching peasants. A cop.

Peasants were given some rights. They could legally gather dead limbs from the tree for fuel, breaking them off "by hook or by crook." It wasn't enough.

By the thirteenth century in Germany there were local regulations restricting the grazing of goats and sheep in cut-over areas to give the trees a chance to come back. Exports

"By hook or by crook."

were forbidden and only dry wood could be used for fuel. Soon it was required that a man plant six oak trees and six fruit trees before he could be married, an early form of management for sustained yield.

In Britain the story was much the same, except more so. Timber use was closely regulated, and the expanding nation was running out of island. The New World turned out to be just the thing for the pocketbooks of the lords and ladies, and for the stomachs of the huddled masses as well.

What they found on this land was a super organism, a full-blown symphony of life. The majesty of an ecosystem at full maturity. A biological civilization of infinite complexity with interrelationships far more intricate than the economies of man and more diverse than the most untouched of the forests of the Old World. Here were trees that had not been seen by Europeans since they were fighting cave bears with rocks.

When the ice ages arrived, the cold moved steadily south across Europe and America, forcing the trees to

move ahead of it. (Trees may be slow but they can outrun a glacier.) In North America the trees made a steady withdrawal to the south, moving down between the two continental mountain ranges to wait until the ice receded. When the warming came, they all moved back north to reclaim their former territories.

The European trees, however, were not so fortunate. As they were forced southward, they found their retreat blocked by a chain of mountain ranges that went from east to west rather than from north to south as in America. The less cold-tolerant trees, such as the hickories and magnolias, died out, leaving postglacial Europe with a short deck.

But the hand of man had been upon this land, however lightly. Though lacking the iron and steel of the Europeans, the native peoples possessed a powerful tool—fire—and they used it to great effect. Although massive, the mature forest produces relatively little food for wildlife and man. The Indians quite deliberately went about modifying the environment to suit their own needs. They opened up great areas by setting fires to kill off the timber overstory.

The sunlight on the soil provided a perfect growing bed for the wild berries that were essential to the diets of both man and beast. Wildlife and human populations grew together. Around the charred stumps of the great trees, saplings sprang up from the still-living root systems. These saplings were of a dimension that could readily be put to use without resort to elaborate technology. Even the great trees were felled with fire by burning them around their waists until they fell. Once down, they were hollowed into canoes by more burning and scraping.

The native population influenced the environment in other ways as well. The black locust tree was not indigenous to the coastal reaches of

Virginia; yet it was found growing there when the first Europeans arrived. This tree had originally been restricted to the Appalachian range of mountains. When the Indians from that area migrated down to the coast, this tree came with them, and it flourished as well. The Indians used black locust wood for hunting bows, but whether the tree made the move as captive or camp follower, we'll never know.

For the first few years, the Europeans were quite unprepared to deal with this new environment. Their primary objective was to get rich quick. Gold being the ultimate measure of wealth, some of the first people to wade ashore were indeed goldsmiths, who were expected to go right to work on the golden shores casting bars to send back to England. When it turned out that the beaches on the western reaches of the Atlantic were as sandy and goldless as those on the eastern side, the settlers turned to the extraction of baser commodities.

One of the resources essential to the well-being of Great Britain was tar and pitch derived from coniferous trees. An island nation, Britain depended on strong merchant and naval fleets for its economic power and military security. Wooden-hulled ships sailed in warm water face an enemy far more destructive than a Spanish man-of-war: ship worms. Unless the hull is protected by a copper sheathing or a pitch coating, the ship worms will destroy it.

Britain's only source for tar and pitch was the Baltic area of northern Europe, an area controlled by Sweden. Unfortunately for Britain, Sweden, which was not always inclined to be friendly to its rival power, could cut off the supply of this strategic commodity at will.

Another source had to be found, and the conifer-rich land of British America looked like just the place. The second boatload of settlers for

Running a small tar pit.

Jamestown included a team of Polish tar experts who began the development of the American naval stores industry. Trees were slashed to produce turpentine and rosin; stumps and knots were burned in smoldering mounds to release the tar and pitch.

Masts were another important resource for the British government. Prime trees were marked with the royal "broad arrow" to claim them as crown property, even if they were on land already appropriated by the colonists. This became an early cause of

friction between the parties involved.

The beginnings of settlement and commerce all up and down the North American coastline were rather shaky at the start. The typical British immigrant was not used to dealing with such massive timber. The ancient cycle of destruction, waste, and shortage would have been repeated more severely than it was if it had not been for the Old World body of laws and traditions regarding conservation that the settlers carried with them. Still, though here and there in short supply,

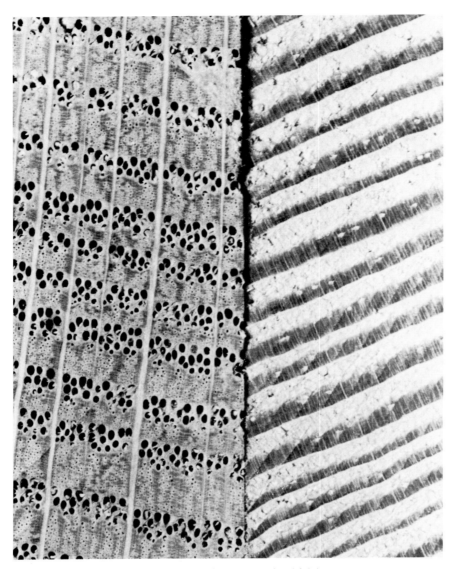

Slow growth makes the red oak (left) weaker; yellow pine (right), stronger.

timber was mainly regarded as a hindrance to agriculture and destroyed. This attitude was reflected in the new usage that the word *lumber* gained in the New World. In the British usage it meant discarded material, cluttered junk. In America this was an apt description of the masses of wood that were always in the way of farmers.

Abundance was not the only unfamiliar condition they had to get used to. Britain's strength was built on oak. Although the New World possessed great oaks of a size and trueness of grain that astounded one and all, the settlers soon discovered that many of the native pines were even stronger. In the ancient forest, where trees were centuries old and hundreds of feet tall, the growth rate of the giant trees was very slow. Consequently, the annual rings formed in this old-growth wood were quite close together.

In pine timber slow growth and tight rings make tough, dense, strong wood, just as you might expect. In oaks, however, the effect is just the opposite. Slow growth in oak makes for weaker, more porous wood of a lower density. The reason for this is that every spring an oak has to put out a new set of leaves before the next tree or it's out of business. To get this mass of vegetation out, massive amounts of water must be run up through new plumbing that forms in the wood each spring. These large vessels form a band of constant width in every growth ring, followed by the denser, stronger wood formed during the summer growing season. The slower an oak tree grows, the closer together these bands of weaker spring wood will be. A slow-grown red oak can become so porous that it appears to be 90 percent nothing.

For this reason, particularly in the South, where the remarkably strong longleaf pine grew, flooring in the oldest houses is of pine. Houses built when the first-growth forest was gone and the vigorous second-growth forest was being cut reflect the changes in the materials: they have floors of oak. Fast-grown pine is weak; fast-grown oak is strong.

Other changes took place as the land became more settled. The control of wildfires in the coastal regions saved mature timber but also began a change in the species composition of the forest. When longleaf pine is in the immature "grass stage" of its first few years, it is often attacked by a fungus that stunts its growth. The annual fires that swept through its range, however, singed off this fungus yet left the young tree unharmed. The fires that came with the Europeans were less frequent but larger, owing to the buildup of fuel. If the fungus didn't get it, the big fires would. The range of the longleaf pine is now considerably smaller than what it once was.

So the land was cleared and the forest retreated. Vast areas were laid waste by charcoal burners to fuel the furnaces of the fledgling iron industry. Farmers felled and fenced and burned. But always the forest crept back. An abandoned field first starts to grow up in broom sedge. Pioneer species that can do well in the open, such as pines, take root and soon cover the sedge and the plow-furrowed clay. The pine may be seeded so thickly from surrounding trees that to survive a tree must grow quick and tall, shedding useless lower branches that are hidden from the sun by the neighboring trees. It is a race to the death because any tree that is left behind in the shade will surely die.

The pines return, straight and tall, in silent warfare with one another. Meanwhile, the wood of the abandoned farmhouse has been slowly making its way down to the soil again through the workings of termites and fungal mycelia. The oak tree that was spared and nurtured by the farmer as a shade tree, though, still grows. Unlike a forest-grown oak, which must grow tall and clear to reach the sun, this tree grew in the open, and its low branches reach out all around, holding its space against the aggressive young pines growing up around it. Its turn is to come, for the pines have changed the space beneath themselves to a shady, protected environment perfect for the growth of young hardwoods. And the acorns are ready.

Through the carpet of needles they break, young oaks and hickories winding their way up to the sun. Each year the pine seeds fall, but unless they land in a clear sunny spot, they will not be able to grow. Every space vacated by a dying pine is seized by the hardwoods, which slowly take over the forest and force out the pines.

Beneath the hardwood canopy, though, there are trees that can live in the shade and never try to reach the top. The forest develops an understory composed of shade-tolerant

Young pines begin to grow amid the broom sedge of the abandoned field.

trees, such as dogwood, holly, and sourwood. The old shade-tree oak may still be living, its spreading branches a clear marker to lead you to the rubble mound of the collapsed chimney and the still-flowering daffodils that speak of the family who came and went.

Other immigrants made their way into the forest. Trees were carried far from their original homes to live as ornaments on the farm. From across the mountains came the Kentucky coffee tree and the Osage orange.

From Asia came the chinaberry and mimosa. They brought with them beauty and disaster.

Around the turn of this century a fungus that was relatively harmless to the oriental chestnut found its way to these shores. This blight, *Endothia parasitica*, was as fatal to our native chestnuts as smallpox had been to the Mandans. The chestnuts died, a devastating shock to the mammal population that had fattened on the sweet nuts for thousands of years.

The effect of this tragedy on man

Hardwoods take hold beneath the pines and will soon become dominant.

The old oak shade tree still remains.

was not nearly as profound as it was on the animals, but it reached us nonetheless. I came across a most touching newspaper story once. The headline read, "Says He Found Cure for Chestnut Blight in Bible." The photo showed a grim but faithful man painting a dying chestnut tree with his concoction of biblical ingredients.

The only cure, though, may be one more ancient than the Scriptures. It is a foolish parasite that kills its host. A fungus can feel foolish only in evolutionary terms, a slow-thinking reaction at best, but the offended tree is reacting too. The odd resistant tree passes on its strength to its young. Through time they will come to live together.

The Trees

In my previous book I talked about most of the species of trees that I work with everyday. I make less frequent use of many of the trees listed in the section to follow, but each has its place in the woodworker's trade.

Aspen *Populus tremuloides*
The quaking aspen is the most widely distributed tree in North America, covering most all of Canada, the northern United States, and the Rocky Mountains. The rounded, heart-shaped leaves flutter in the slightest breeze. They are fast growing but short lived, moving quickly

into areas that have been cleared by logging or fire. After a few decades, other species will become dominant where the aspen grove once stood. Aspens rot out very quickly and are a great source of food for beavers and deer. When the tree is cut, new sprouts shoot up from the roots, forming a grove composed of trees of the same genetic makeup. The wood is light, soft, and weak but easy to work. It shrinks very little on seasoning. Aspens make good log houses provided they are protected from the ground.

Aspens drop their lower branches, leaving eyelike scars on the white bark.

White cedars are straight and tall with scalelike leaves similar to red cedar.

Black gums are among the first to turn scarlet in the fall.

Atlantic white-cedar
Chamaecyparis thyoides

This increasingly scarce tree grows along the Atlantic and Gulf coasts of the United States. It is sometimes found in pure stands, or "glades." This is the tree that was mined from bogs; the huge logs remained sound beneath the water for centuries. John Lawson described the tree well in 1708. "As strait as an Arrow," he called it. "It is extraordinary light, and free to rive. 'Tis good for Yard, Top-Masts, Booms and Boltsprits, being very tough. The best Shingles for Houses are made of this Wood, it being no Strain to the Roof, and never rots. Good Pails and other Vessels free from Leakage, are likewise made therof. The Bark of this and the red Cedar, the Indians use to make their Cabins of, which prove firm, and resist all Weathers."

A cypress in Lake Mattamuskeet.

Bald cypress *Taxodium distichum*

This landmark tree of the southern swamps is one of the few coniferous trees that shed their needles in the winter. The buttressed stump and "knees" that protrude from the water make it quite distinctive. It is a slow-growing tree that can reach huge sizes, as it lives for centuries. The wood of the cypress is relatively resistant to decay. For this reason it is valuable for construction in high-humidity locations, such as greenhouses and water tanks. It rives well with the growth rings and makes excellent roof shingles. A coffin made from this wood will last a lifetime.

Black gum *Nyssa sylvatica*

The black gum, or tupelo, ranges throughout the eastern states. It is a medium-sized tree found in many different forest environments. In some regions it is an important tree for the production of honey. In the fall the smooth-sided oval leaves turn a brilliant red. The wood is not durable in contact with the soil. Old trunks frequently rot out hollow and serve as homes for honey bees. The wood is hard and heavy but rather weak. It is used for wagon hubs, construction timbers, and woodenware. It has a beautiful brown color and turns well on a lathe. "This Tree (the Indians report) is never wounded by Lightning. It has no certain Grain; and it is almost impossible to split or rive it" (Lawson, 1708).

Box *Buxus sp.*

Heavy, hard, and dense, boxwood is the ivory of trees. In fact it is so valuable that it is sold by weight rather than by volume. The small trees are cultivated as ornamentals, which are my major source of supply. It is a choice wood for the finest carving and turnery and will take and hold a razor-sharp edge. It is used for engraving, scientific instruments, rulers, and inlay work. One familiar use

is for the wear strips inset into the bottoms of woodworking planes. Box is not exceptionally more difficult to season than other woods, but since it is only available in small pieces and is often used for turnery in the full round stem, slow drying for several years is the only way to avoid the otherwise inevitable radial cracks.

Buckeye *Aesculus sp.*

Buckeyes have distinctive upright pyramidal clusters of flowers and palmately compound leaves (the five to seven leaflets fan out from a common center). The large, glossy brown nuts that give this tree its name are held in thick husks until they ripen. These seeds are reported to be toxic, but when kept in your pocket, they are supposed to ward off rheumatism. The introduced ornamental horse chestnut is another species of buckeye. These last are quite widespread, while the native species grow mainly in the central and eastern mountain

states. The buckeye is one of the first trees to put out its leaves in the spring. The light-colored, soft, lightweight wood is used for woodenware, toys, artificial limbs, drawing boards, and the wooden parts of trunks and valises

Butternut *Juglans cinerea*

This tree of the Midwest and New England states is also commonly known as white walnut. Like that of its cousin the black walnut, the pith of the twigs of the white walnut is chambered with tiny dark diaphragms. White walnut trees can be distinguished from black walnuts by their longer, pecanlike nuts and the wide flat plates of the bark. The tree is short-lived and seldom gets very big. The wood is light in weight and color and is soft and coarse, but it takes a good polish. Its main use is in interior trim and furniture work. The nuts are good to eat, and the husks will make yellow or orange dye for cloth.

This boxwood is from a grove over two centuries old.

Buckeye leaves are palmately compound.

Butternut leaves look like those of black walnut, but the bark has light plates in the young trees.

Catalpa *Catalpa sp.*
Although the two native species of catalpa were once more restricted in range, they have been widely planted and naturalized throughout the eastern half of the country. The heart-shaped leaves, showy flowers, and elongated seed capsules make it a popular ornamental. It is a fast-growing tree and can adapt to many soil conditions and climates. Seasoned catalpa heartwood is quite resistant to decay. It is not generally used commercially, but the rapid growth rate and decay resistance prompt farmers to plant them in groves to grow their own fenceposts. This tree is sometimes called the "cigar tree" or "indian cigar" from the shape of the fruit capsule.

Chinaberry *Melia azedarach*
This naturalized tree from the Orient is the archetype shade tree in working-class yards in the rural South. The yellow fruit is poisonous if eaten, but the hard pits are made into rosary beads. The leaves are double compound with numerous sawtooth-edged leaflets. The chinaberry is the heartiest member of the mahogany family and is known under various local names as such. The trees are fast growing but short-lived. The moderately hard and strong wood is reddish and yellowish brown striped. It is used locally for interior trim and for cabinetmaking.

Cottonwood *Populus sp.*
These fast-growing trees get their name from the tufts of white hairs that float the ripened seeds through the air. Cottonwoods grow best on moist, well-drained soil and are a common sight along river banks. The wood is weak and soft and difficult to season without warping. It is used for musical instruments, berry boxes, and large packing crates. It is also a good wood for tubs and pails for containing food. The people of the Southwest carved religious figures from the roots. Cottonwood burned in a woodstove is reputed to clean the chimney from the buildup of soot caused by burning pine.

Fir *Abies sp.*
The firs live in cold, moist areas of the country. Their needles are flat in cross-section, and their cones are upright on the branches. The wood is rather light, soft, and weak but adequate for general construction purposes. It is free from objectionable odors and is good for food containers like cheese boxes and butter tubs. Fir finds its way into mill-work shops where it is made into sash, doors, and trim. Resin pockets under the bark are the source for the Canada balsam used for cementing the cover glass on microscope slides.

Holly *Ilex opaca*
This tree of the southeastern forests has long been more important for its

Catalpa leaves turn bright yellow in early fall.

Chinaberries often grow in a characteristic umbrella shape.

Cottonwood leaves are heart shaped like those of aspens.

Fir needles are flat with two light-colored bands on their undersides.

American holly can reach 100 feet high and 4 feet in diameter.

ritual uses than for its structural uses. The name *holly* appears to derive from the word *holy*. Its bright green leaves and scarlet fruit have attracted religious types since ancient Greece. Holly trees are very tolerant of shade and are a common component of the understory of mature southern forests. The wood is tough, but light and weak. It is close grained and ivory white and is used for furniture inlay, engravings, scientific instrument scales, and, when died black to imitate ebony, piano keys. It works well on a lathe and makes "good Trenchers and other Turnery-ware" (Lawson).

Honey locust *Gleditsia triacanthos*
The honey locust is easy to spot even in the winter by its platy grey-brown bark bearing armaments of sharp multipronged spines. These spines were once called "confederate pins," as they were used to hold the shirts on soldiers who had no material or time to replace lost buttons. These trees are widespread but relatively scarce. The leaves are pinnately or bipinnately compound, composed of up to twenty-eight leaflets. Cattle love to eat the sweet seed pods, and since the seeds pass through the animals undigested, the trees are spread wherever they roam. Honey locust wood is quite heavy, hard, strong, stiff, and difficult to work. The wood is very attractive and interesting but little used, since commercial quantities are not available. Locally it is used for wagon hubs and fencing. It is moderately resistant to decay, but not to the extent that black locust is.

Kentucky coffee tree
Gymnocladus dioicus
A member of the pea family, this native of the central states was popular at one time as an ornamental and has spread eastward beyond its original range. Its seeds were once roasted for use as a coffee substitute; the raw

Spineless forms of honey locust are often cultivated, but are rare in the wild.

These Kentucky coffee-tree leaves had already turned yellow in mid-September.

An old ship's knee leans against this live oak on Roanoke Island.

Magnolia trees are easy to climb.

The broken limbs on this pear tree were caused by over-abundant fruit production.

seeds, however, are poisonous. The scientific name means "naked branch," a reference to the brief time in the summer that the leaves are out. When they are out, though, the leaves are huge, up to 3 feet long and 2 feet wide. The leaves are bipinnately compound, meaning that they are composed of small leaflets on a twice-forking axis. The wood is a warm brown and finishes well for furniture. Being a relatively small and scattered tree, it rarely reaches the market but is used locally for everything from fenceposts to firewood.

Live oak *Quercus virginiana*
The live oak, native to the coastal regions of the southeastern United States, holds its leaves throughout the year—hence its name. With their widespreading crowns and small glossy leaves live oaks are easy to recognize. They grow fast, can live for as long as three centuries, and are such prolific root sprouters that they are next to impossible to kill. Live oak

wood is very hard to cure and work, but it was essential for shipbuilding and blocks for rigging. Lawson wrote of live oak wood: "The Firmness and great Weight therof, frightens our Sawyers from the Fatigue that attends the cutting of this Timber. A Nail once driven therein, 'tis next to an Impossibility to draw it out. The Limbs therof are so curved, that they serve for excellent Timbers, Knee, etc. for Vessels of any sort."

Magnolia *Magnolia sp.*
There are several species of magnolia. The two most common are the cucumber tree of the mountains, whose light, soft, decay-resistant wood is used like tulip poplar for troughs, woodenware, and pump logs, and the southern magnolia, which is harder and heavier. Both are used for joinery work, such as sash, doors, trim, and venetian blinds. The cucumber tree is the only magnolia with a rough, furrowed bark. Both are popular as landscape trees well

into the northern states. Magnolias were among the first trees to evolve the reproductive strategy of developing flowers. Their conelike aggregate fruits bear testimony to the ancient design. Goats and kids can easily climb the ladderlike branches within the cone of foliage.

Pear *Pyrus communis*
This native of Europe has been cultivated since ancient times. It is widely naturalized near inhabited areas throughout the eastern and southern states and in the Northwest. Fruit production can be so heavy that the trees break under the weight. The light brown wood is excellent for the pattern maker who requires a stable, even-grained, easy-to-work material. The earliest surviving scientific instrument made in America is a backstaff made of pear in 1676. Pear is the characteristic wood of the French provincial cabinetmaker. It is beautiful stuff for carving and turnery.

Red mulberry leaves take several different forms.

This Paulownia is only about a dozen years old.

Spruce cones are pendant on the branches.

Red mulberry *Morus rubra*

This native mulberry was joined by two other species, the white and paper mulberries, in colonial times when the hope of building a domestic silkworm industry was keen. The silkworms didn't survive, but the trees did and are now widely naturalized. The red mulberry is a rather small tree, seldom reaching over 50 feet tall. The yellow-orange wood of red mulberry is light, soft, and weak but highly resistant to decay. There is a house near where my father was born where all the window trim is red mulberry. The fruit ripens just after the strawberries and is very sweet. "This tree grows extraordinary round and pleasant to the eye. . . . A very fine Shade, to sit under in the Summertime" (Lawson, 1708).

Royal Paulownia
Paulownia tomentosa

A naturalized native of the Orient named for the Russian princess Anna Paulonia, this tree is also unusual in

It's rare to see flowering sourwood without honeybees around.

that it bears large clusters of blue flowers. Paulownias, or princess trees as they are sometimes called, grow quickly and can spring up in just about any waste area. I once grew a bit suspicious of this tree because it seemed to favor close proximity to broadcast transmitters and large industrial sites. In the fall the clusters of seed pods look like oversized bunches of grapes. The wood is light and soft and easy to work and is much prized in Japan for making furniture and sandals.

Sourwood *Oxydendrum arboreum*

Sometimes known as the sorrel, the sourwood is a common understory component of southeastern hardwood forests. The sour leaves are often chewed by woodsmen to allay thirst. These leaves are among the first to turn scarlet in the late summer. Bees often seek out the white flowers, which resemble lilies of the valley, and make from their nectar a highly prized honey. These flowers bloom

Sweet gum leaves are star shaped; the bark of young trees can be mistaken for white oak in winter.

The branches of white pines form characteristic whorls.

White pine *Pinus strobus, P. monticola*

White pines have their needles in bundles of fives, in contrast to the twos and threes of the hard yellow pines. They are easy to spot from a distance by the whorls of branches formed around the trunk each year. These trees are native to the cooler parts of the country, but are widely planted as ornamentals. Open-grown ornamentals will not shed their lower branches, with the result that their wood is quite knotty. White pine from the forest, though, is clear and even grained and lacks the hard and soft annual rings of yellow pine. The wood is light and soft and nails without splitting. Its primary uses are for boxes, mill work, pattern making, construction timbers, toys, and woodenware.

throughout the summer. The light yellow or pinkish brown wood is very hard, heavy, and close grained. It takes a beautiful polish and is used locally for turnery, tool handles, machine bearings, and sled runners.

Spruce *Picea sp.*

Spruces grow in the colder climates of the continent. The needles are much shorter than those of the pine and grow out on all sides of the stem. These needles are square in cross-section and will roll easily between your fingers. Spruce wood is light and relatively soft, but quite strong and elastic. These characteristics suit it particularly well for such special purposes as ladder rails, oars and paddles, boats, and general construction. Spruce is the wood of preference in making the sound boards of musical instruments. The Sitka spruce is particularly valuable for its high strength-to-weight ratio and is used in aircraft construction. I made a new propeller for my old power-generating windmill from this tree.

Sweet gum *Liquidambar styraciflua*

Sweet gums get to be big trees. Common in the South, they are easy to recognize by the star-shaped leaves, the prickly seed balls, and corky "wings" on the twigs. The sapwood is white, frequently tainted pink or blue. The heartwood is reddish brown, but is formed in usable quantities only in trees over 16 inches thick. The wood rots quickly in contact with the ground, but turns beautifully on a lathe. "The sweet Gum-Tree, so call'd, because of the fragrant Gum it yields in the spring-time, upon Incision of the Bark, or Wood. It cures the Herpes and Inflammations; being apply'd to the Morphew and Tettars. 'Tis an extraordinary Balsam, and of great Value to those who know how to use it. No wood has scarce a better grain; wherof fine Tables, Drawers, and other Furniture might be made. Some of it is curiously curl'd" (Lawson, 1708).

HELVES AND HANDLES

First she gave him a great axe of bronze.
Its double blade was sharpened well, and the shapely handle
of olive wood fixed firmly in its head was
fitted to his grip.

Homer, *The Odyssey* (800 B.C.)

Held and worked directly with the hand, the first tools of stone and bone depended on the limited velocity that could be achieved within the swing of the arm. Slowly man began to extend his reach and thereby his grasp and power with throwing sticks and stone axes bound to handles of antler or wood. This lengthening by the addition of the helve greatly increased the distance over which the stone axe could be accelerated and at the same time isolated the body from the shock of impact.

Connecting the stone and the wood securely enough to withstand the tremendous shock is a challenge that has remained with us to this day. The makers of the earliest axes inserted the fractured flint into the cleft end of a stick. Each blow, though, wedged the stick apart, thus limiting the force that could be applied.

Other axe makers worked a furrow around the stone axe head, bent the tapered wood of the helve around in this seat, and bound the whole thing with rawhide. I have used a stone axe hafted in this manner to fell trees. (It worked well, but I am not sure whether this particular axe head was intended for woodworking or for combat. I may have been doing the Stone Age equivalent of trying to fell timber with a halberd borrowed from the Swiss Guards.)

The next step was the development of socket axes of cast bronze. By making the hole in the axe head rather than the handle, the horse was finally put before the cart. These socket axes were mounted on naturally L-shaped hafts. Reset on the haft with a 90-degree axial rotation such an axe head became an adze.

The socket axe relieved the splitting problem, but it was soon superseded by another prehistoric pattern from the land of Ur. In this design the handle was secured in a hole through the head at right angles to the direc-

Stone axe with a hickory haft.

tion of the action. In spite of the troublesome tendency of such axes to "fly off the handle" from the centrifugal force of the swing, this force is considerably less disruptive than the tangential displacement caused by impact and withdrawal. In other words, try and think of a better way to do it.

Although the axe head has changed from stone to copper, to bronze, and then to iron and steel, the helve, aside from a Mesolithic prelude with antler, has always been of wood. There is simply no other material that will do the job as well. And although the bronze axe that Calypso gave to Odysseus was hafted in olive wood (they were on an island in the Mediterranean), the wood of choice for the European was ash. Tough and resilient, ash is flexible enough to give

some "whip" to the stroke, yet strong enough to withstand the tremendous stresses that this occupation entails.

Ash reigned unchallenged until the Europeans made their way across the Atlantic. The ash of the New World, particularly southern varieties, was considered to be of poorer quality. Small matter though, because hickory, which was unknown in Britain, was found to be even better. The hickory-versus-ash debate has been long fought, but the difference is not all that great. There is a bit of chauvinism operating here. After all, ash is a sacred tree of ancient Europe. Hickory, comparatively, has no background at all. A few years ago a carpenter friend, a Basque, made a pilgrimage to work in his hometown of Bilbao, Spain, for a few months. He

Hickory for helves.

Rive the blanks with a froe.

floor is often perforated with hidden "pine holes," where old stumps have rotted out. If you step in one, your foot goes down about 10 inches before it hits bottom. When this happens to you with a hundred and fifty pounds of hickory on your shoulder, you can get hurt.

Whether you split the log in the woods to lighten the load or wait until you get home, don't let it linger very long unbarked and unriven. Bugs love to get in under hickory bark, and the longer you leave it on, the harder it is to get off. If you leave the log too long the bark will rot free or be eaten off by the bugs and the log will be too far gone to use. If you wait too long to split the log, it will not only be harder to do but the log will be more prone to damage from seasoning checks as well.

Split the log first radially into eighths or sixteenths and then tangentially to remove the very narrow sharp end of the pie-shaped pieces. You will find that hickory splits well in either direction. The object here is to prepare straight-grained billets large enough to make handles from but small enough to season within a reasonable time. I prefer to orient the grain of an axe helve so that the growth rings run at right angles to its width, bark side toward the poll, heart side to the bit. If the growth rings are oriented in line with the direction of the swing, the helve will occasionally develop an undesirable curve to the side. Stick the billets up in the loft and forget about them for a year.

took his new American rubber-grip framing hammer with him. When the other carpenters saw it, though, they laughed and threw nails at him and gave him such a hard time that he could not use it the whole time he was there. Working men are a conservative lot.

Making Helves

Start by locating a hickory (or ash or white oak) tree about 8 or so inches thick that has a clear, knot-free length of at least 3 feet. Cut it down and examine the growth rings. Slow-grown wood with abnormally close rings (say less than 1/16 inch) is apt to be too brittle for the roughest use. Handles are best made from second-growth stock that has grown more rapidly than the trees found in the first cutting of a forest.

Axe helves are traditionally made from the lighter-colored sapwood of the tree rather than from the darker wood of the heart. The grade of

commercial axe handles was often determined by the proportion of light sapwood to dark heartwood they contained The highest grade of stock is solid white. The reasoning behind this is partially the rate of growth.

As the tree grows, new rings of living sapwood are added each year. Within a finite number of years the cells of the sapwood build up deposits of what are called "extractives," cease their biological functioning, and become heartwood. If the tree has been growing fast enough, the total width of the growth rings in the sapwood will be enough to make axe handles from. In a slow-growing tree, the total width of these sapwood rings will be quite narrow, and an axe handle made from it, besides being brittle, will of necessity contain some darker heartwood. This heartwood is often more difficult to season without checking. The width of the sapwood would be greater in a better tree.

Hickory is very heavy, and a double-helve length—6 feet long—can easily be too much to carry any distance out of the woods. The forest

Shaping

When L-shaped sticks became obsolete, axemen turned to straight shafts of cleft wood and stayed with them until quite recently. The axe that began the felling of the great forest of America is quite different from the

Helve styles (from left): straight, my own, commercial fawn's foot.

This pattern is as long as from my nose to the tip of my outstretched arm.

one that finished the job. In the nineteenth century, axe handles began to take on the familiar S curve that they retain to this day. The S curve tends to direct the axe as you swing. The butt end of the helve which formerly ended in a simple square cut, began growing the diagonally truncated swell that is commonly known as the fawn's foot. Some of the popularity of this new pattern can be attributed to the rise of power repeating lathes, which could turn out such pieces in mass quantities, but the most exaggerated examples of this genre were definitely handmade. Freed from the strictures of the straight line, the axeman found a new way to express himself.

I keep a curved, modified fawn's-foot pattern in quarter-inch pine for nineteenth- and twentieth-century axes. The straight pattern for earlier and double-bitted axes comes to me extempore at the shaving horse. Take the blank down out of the loft and shave or plane two sides flat and straight. Set the pattern on one side and trace around it. With the hatchet

chop down close to the outline. Now go back to the shaving horse or handle vise and shave true to the line with the drawknife. On the slopes of curved handles, you must of course do all your cutting with the grain. This simply means that you must shave only downslope. The drawknife can do it all, but a spokeshave is certainly a help. Remember that hickory will tear out in the grain unless it is well seasoned. Dry hickory responds to the spokeshave beautifully, leaving a glossy, ivorylike surface.

As the final shape approaches, test the size with your hand. The tip of your thumb should just pass the first knuckle of your index finger. Slide the axe handle through your hand as though you were felling a tree and keep sighting down it to make sure that everything looks and feels as it should. Shape the head end down to just over the size that would fit into the eye of the axe head and saw a slot lengthwise down its end for the wedge. Go over the whole of the helve with a piece of broken glass used as a scraper. Then put it away

again in a dry place for as long as you can stand it (months or weeks—I know how it is). The head end of the helve should be very dry before you fit it up.

Out with the Old

Sometimes getting the old handle out is tougher than getting the new one in. The easiest way to get a broken axe handle out is to saw it off flush on the underside of the head and drive it out with a wooden drift.

Often, though, the eye of the axe is flared at both ends, and it's as tough to drive it out one way as it is the other. In such a case, you can bore a series of holes in the underside, being careful not to hit any metal wedges with the auger. You can then break the wood into the middle and drive it out.

Another approach is to soak the wooden handle in water. The swelling wood will be crushed by the confining metal, so that when you place the axe

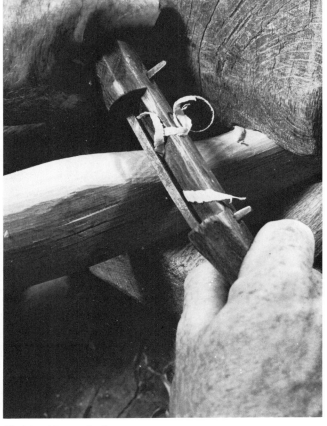

Shape with a drawknife on a shaving horse.   *Finish with a spokeshave.*

in the oven at 200 degrees, the wood will shrink up and be easy to remove.

If nothing else works, you can try burning the old handle out, but you must be careful to keep the cutting edge from getting too hot, which would destroy the temper. To protect the temper, bury the business end of the axe head in moist earth and build a fire around the eye. For double-bitted axes you must cover both bits in the damp earth and build a fire in a trough dug under the eye.

Hanging

As Homer well knew, the fit of the handle to the head is a critical point. The head must be perfectly aligned as well as secure on the helve. Start by shaving just the end quarter inch of the helve to fit tight in the eye of the head. Set the head on the handle just this far and, holding the foot end, hang the axe like a plumb bob and sight down to see that the bit is directly in line with the center of the foot.

You also need to determine how "open" or "closed" you want the axe head to be. To check this hold the axe on a flat surface so that the foot of the helve and the cutting edge both touch. Usually the axe head is set so that the edge touches the flat surface at a point between one-third and one-half the way up from the inside corner. The further up the bit toward the top end that contact is made, the more acute the angle between the head and the helve and the more closed the head is hanging. A slightly more closed axe (as I have mine) works better for hewing logs in the stand-on-top-and-chop-down-below-your-feet mode. If you get the axe hanging as you want it now, you can easily see and make the adjustments necessary to maintain that angle as the fitting process proceeds.

With the head set properly on the last quarter inch of the helve, examine the eye and the helve closely to see what wood you need to remove to maintain the alignment as the helve is driven home. The eye of the axe may not be exactly in line with its bit, so look carefully. You can live with a slightly more open or closed axe, but the edge alignment with the helve is critical. An error of 3 degrees is too much.

To drive the helve into the head, hold the foot end of the helve with the

Assuming the feet of their helves both touch the same plane as the bits, the axe on the left is hung more closed than the one on the right.

head hanging down and strike the end of the foot with a mallet. Here's where a pointy fawn's foot is a real nuisance, and is usually sawn off. The inertia of the iron axe head will allow the helve to be driven in without having to set the head up against anything. When the helve protrudes from the top end of the eye, take a wedge made from a suitably hard wood (although some people prefer softer wood like poplar, feeling that it will grip better) and drive it into the slot. Cross this wooden wedge with an iron one driven in at right angles to the first.

Keeping It On

If you do the job carefully to begin with, there will be no play to cause further wear in the helve. Once the head gets loose, though, it keeps working looser and becomes a hazard to you and those around you. If the head shows signs of moving, drive in another iron wedge—a real one, not a nail.

Never try to tighten an axe or any other handle by sticking it in water to make the wood swell up. This works so well the first time that you do it that the fibers of the wood are permanently crushed by being forced against the unyielding iron walls. When the handle dries out, it shrinks up smaller than it was when you began. This is a good way to remove

an old handle as well as to ruin a new one.

Remember that leaving an axe out in the rain or even standing for a while in wet grass will have the same effect. The linseed oil usually rubbed into the wood is not an effective moisture barrier. Keeping it dry is part of taking care of your axe.

Broad Axes

Because a broad axe is used in sweeping strokes down across the side of a recumbent timber, its handle must be bent to one side to maintain enough clearance to leave the skin attached to your knuckles as you work. On early or Germanic broad axes the eye is elongated and directed to one side

Drive in the helve. The helve next to the one being driven has bent because its growth rings were oriented tangentially.

Drive in the wedge.

or the other. Such an axe can take a straight helve and is forged to be either right or left handed. (Right- or left-handed use refers to which hand you place forward as you work.) Broad axe handles are generally made short (24 inches or so) because the heads are heavy and the common broad axe stroke is a short sweep down across the grain of a log.

The bend is obtained either by actually bending the wood while it is still green or after steaming or by shaping the wood as the handle is made. I prefer the latter approach, and I often set aside pieces of hickory that have grain that follows the general shape I want. Broad axes do not

have to endure the stresses that felling axes do, and it is less important that the grain follow the form exactly. Just as a personal preference, I like the helve to bend out away from the eye and then return to be more or less parallel to the blade.

Adze Handles

The blade of an adze sits at right angles to that of an axe. In addition, the handle is inserted from the opposite end of the head and is made to be easily removed. The reason for this last is immediately apparent when

it is time to grind the blade. An axe blade can be ground on a grindstone with the handle in place, but with an adze, which is sharpened only on its inner face, the handle gets in the way. The solution was to make the adze head easily removable. The eye in the head is tapered so that the handle will slip through until it reaches a similarly tapered end.

Adze handles have undergone an evolution similar to that of axe handles. Earlier examples were relatively straight; they began taking on the S curve in the nineteenth century. The process of selecting wood and shaping is the same as for axes. A good length for adze handles is from

Shaping a broad axe helve.

your nose to the wrist of your out-stretched arm. The head must again be perfectly aligned with the helve, this time of course at right angles.

The degree of openness or closed-ness may again be determined by setting the adze on a flat surface so that both the blade and the foot end of the helve make contact. On a pin poll adze (one with a narrow hammer point on the back end) the blade should hit the same point as the center of the pin poll does when the adze is rotated. On flat poll adzes you want the blade to hit at a point about a half inch in from the top end of the poll. An adze that is set at too obtuse an angle to the handle will tend to dig

into the wood, too acute an angle will glance off the wood and dig into your leg.

Socket Chisels

On a chisel the direction of the action is in line with the handle, making the socket arrangement entirely agree-able. From the seventeenth to the nineteenth centuries there was a change in the design of the socket, though. During the earlier time most were hexagonal, while later chisel sockets are conical. The handles for the latter are readily turned out in

quantity on lathes, but the former are more easily made by hand. When chisels were sold unhandled, this was an important difference.

I doubt if you will encounter very many hexagonal socket chisels in your rambles, but conical socket tools abound. Many of them are damaged by being used without a handle and struck with a steel hammer rather than with a mallet. The damaged socket can usually be restored by heating and reforging on the horn of the anvil.

I make my turned handles of sea-soned hickory, taking careful mea-surements with inside and outside calipers so that the fit will be over-sized just enough to stay tight. This means that the wood should fit in hand tight to within ⅛ inch of the turned shoulder and is then driven in the rest of the way. You can check for any tight spots by test fitting and shaving away any places indicated by the discoloration of contact with the metal.

Chisels subjected to heavy use may need the support of an iron ring at the striking end. This ring can be either forged from an iron strip and welded or hacksawn from a length of iron pipe. Turn the seat to receive this ring on the end of the handle and remove it from the lathe. Drive the ring on and put the whole affair back in the lathe and smooth the rough corners with a file as the metal spins.

Tanged Handles

Tanged handles, where the wood is driven onto a spikelike extension of the tool, are among the toughest to do right. Since the metal is contained by the wood rather than the other way around, splitting is a persistent problem. Most such tools are limited to lighter duty. The chisels and gouges

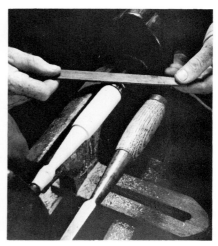

Smooth the ring with a file as the handle spins on the lathe.

Double exposure of the same adze rotated shows correct hanging.

of cabinetmakers, turners, joiners and carvers commonly have tanged handles, as do drawknives and other tools that are pulled rather than pushed.

With a properly prepared hole the tapered tang will fit tightly without splitting the wood. Tangs are usually tapered square and can sometimes be successfully driven into a prebored hole without damage. To lower the odds of splitting the handle, it can be left oversized and then shaped down to the finished dimensions after the tang is in place. If the tool end of the handle is ringed with an iron or brass ferrule, again the problem is greatly diminished. This helps to preserve the tool in use as well.

Two other approaches are to soften the wood within the hole by filling it with water for a few minutes or to burn the prebored hole to the proper size by heating the tang and forcing it into the wood. When you burn-set a handle, stop about a quarter inch from home (less on smaller handles), pull the tang out, and pour water in the hole. This should leave just enough of a force fit to set the tang firm without a split.

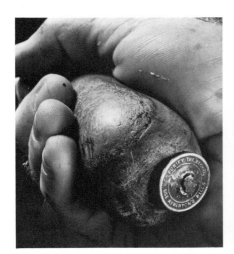

You find strange things on drawknife handles.

One sort of tanged tool does, in a way, have the action at right angles to the handle. T-handle twist augers, from tiny gimlets to great 3-inch barn framers, will often have a broad flat tang rather than a barrel eye through which the handle passes. The flatness of the tang is intended to use the grain of the wooden handle to its best advantage. The flat tang is set through at right angles to the length of the handle so that the force from twisting is exerted along the grain rather than across it. A tang set in along the grain would split the handle along its length the first time you used it.

Saw Handles

Many of the earliest saw handles were tanged, and some light-duty ones still are. Gradually, though, the tang and bent-wood handle were supplanted by a similar pistol-grip style that was slotted to allow the blade to be sandwiched within the wood and secured by bolts or rivets. Beech is the preferred wood for this, as it takes the sculpturing well without fracturing. Through the eighteenth century, this open-grip, dolphin-tail

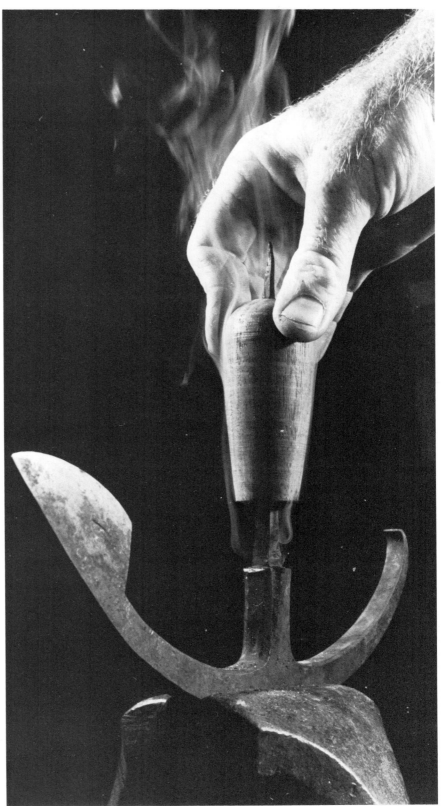

Burn-setting a handle on a hurdle maker's twivil.

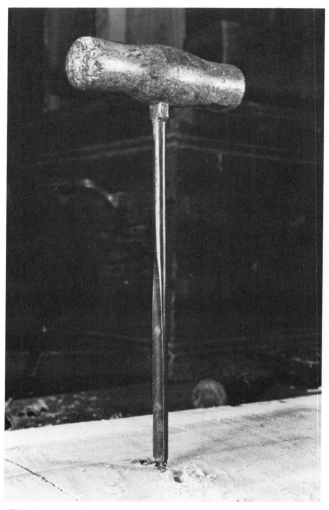

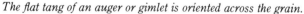

The flat tang of an auger or gimlet is oriented across the grain.

Modern saw handles from different makers show the integration of the pistol grip to the hollow grip.

handle began to grow a return at its base that led to the common hollow-grip handle in use today. You can plainly trace the integration of this return into the design from the graceful buttress of the earlier saws to the all but rectangular block with a hand-hole in it that is used today.

The only saw handle that I have had occasion to make was a replace-ment for a termite-eaten one-man crosscut saw. It was rather like a large handsaw handle, and replacing it was a simple matter of copying the remains of what was there before. One-man crosscut saws often have an auxiliary handle that can be mounted either above the regular one for a two-handed grip or on the far end of the blade for assistance from a willing

other. An internal screw thread that tightens or loosens the grip as the handle is twisted makes this handle easy to remove and reset. This sort of handle is relatively modern, quite useful, and not something that you would usually make for yourself.

Two-man crosscut saws from the late nineteenth century also have han-dles that can do tricks, many of them

A one-man crosscut with auxilliary handle; a four-position two-man crosscut handle in the background.

The log-rolling cant hook needs all the strength of its grain.

patented. These handles can be set at right angles to the blade for felling the tree. Then, by loosening a wing nut, they can be set back in line with the blade for bucking the tree (cutting it into lengths) once it is down. The same wing nut attachment allows the handle to be removed entirely so that the saw can be pulled endwise from the kerf, rather than backed out the

way it went in. This feature quickly shows its usefulness when the kerf is blocked by wedges driven in to keep it open or has closed up on its own.

The language of the tools can be as eloquent as that of Shakespeare. I have an old cant hook which I treasure. Where the iron hook passes through the oak handle, the grain of the wood flows around the slot and

returns unbroken on the other side. The maker of this cant hook cut the slot right where a knot had been. The grain of the growing oak passed around the knot like a gentle river around a rock. Rather than weaken the cant hook, the knot gave it the strength to endure where others would have failed. "Sweet are the uses of adversity."

SAWS

When Workmen light of a good Blade . . .
they matter not much whether the Teeth be sharp or deep,
or set to their mind: For to make them so, is a
Task they take to themselves.

Joseph Moxon, *Mechanick Exercises* (1678)

Bow saws.

Our Neolithic ancestors had a problem: how to harvest grain without knocking the seed loose from the heads. They had no metalworking, and thus no long, sharp knives. Their stone knives were sharper than razors but limited in length. The solution was to fix a number of these sharp stone blades along a length of bone or wood. A sheaf of grain could be taken in hand and cleanly cut by drawing this array of blades across the stalks. This was the beginning of the saw.

As the knowledge of metalworking progressed, so did the saw, which now became a tool for woodworking as well. Ancient copper and bronze saws followed the pattern of the Neolithic sickle, in that they were worked primarily on the pull stroke. The earliest metals were too weak to work well on the push stroke without buckling, and these ancient blades had no "set," a defect that left them prone to binding in the kerf.

The first reference we have to setting the teeth on a saw—that is, bending the teeth alternately "to the right and left in turn" so that the saw kerf will be wider than the thickness of the blade—is from the first-century A.D. Roman historian Pliny. He even comments that sawing green wood requires more set in the saw than dry wood—something that you may have experienced for yourself.

Bow Saws

Another device that was well developed by the Roman period was the use of a wooden frame to hold the blade taut as it was worked through the wood. A blade held in such an arrangement could not only be worked on a push stroke but could also be made quite narrow in both thickness and width, making it a lot cheaper and easier to make.

In Continental Europe bow saws are still preferred to the broad-bladed handsaw. They are easy to use and versatile in that the narrow blade can readily cut curves or openings in the middle of a board. I make my own saws and use them for cutting everything from logs to tiny dovetails. They are pretty things as well.

A bow saw has three major wooden parts: the two upright ends and the middle stretcher. The blade is fixed into the base of the two uprights, and several lengths of cord are strung between their tops. Turning a toggle stick placed through the cords twists and shortens them, levering the uprights against the fulcrum of the stretcher and further straining and stiffening the blade. The toggle stick is held by catching it against the stretcher. When the saw is not in use, the tension should be let off by allowing the toggle to unwind a bit. (Put a stone on the free end of the toggle as you let it go and you have a miniature "onager," a siege weapon also used by the Romans. Another military spinoff.) More modern bow saws from the last two centuries often use threaded metal rods and a turnbuckle to tighten the blade, but the principle and the admonition to loosen it up when you're done remain the same.

You can make a bow saw in an afternoon. You can even make the blade yourself, following the instructions given elsewhere in this chapter. Assuming you have a blade, or the steel to make one from, begin by drawing a full-sized pattern of the saw you want to make on a board or on the ground to use as a reference as you work.

I make my bow saw frames from hickory, although beech or hard maple are the more commonly used woods. Split flat billets from a clear log, trace the outlines of the pieces on their sides, and chop and shave down to the finished shape. It's the same process that you go through making

axe handles, roughing out in the green wood and finishing up as the wood seasons. (The afternoon is a cumulative one, spread over several months.)

Continental bow saws typically have the stretcher notched in a U-shaped yoke on both ends to cradle the midpoints of the uprights. The Anglo-American practice uses a stretcher set into mortices cut into the uprights. Chop this mortice with a chisel that is the same width as the stretcher tenons by systematically driving it in across the grain, advancing it about an eighth of an inch each time down the length of the mortice. When you have done one run, turn the bevel of the chisel around and go back the way you came, removing the chips as you go. A half inch deep is quite enough.

The blade, or "web," for a crosscutting bow saw is set in slots sawn into the bottoms of the uprights and held in place by metal pins. If you make a saw with a downwardly extended upright to form a handle, you must make the slot through this piece by first drilling a hole at each end of where the slot is to go and then taking out the intervening wood with a coping or keyhole saw.

If you are making a turning or rip saw, however, you will need a different blade attachment, one that will allow the blade to be rotated and held in any direction along its longitudinal axis. A turning saw, as its name indicates, is intended to cut tight turns and curves in the wood. To keep the body of the saw clear from the sides of the piece being cut, the blade must have some means of being reoriented at angles other than straight ahead.

The same is true with a rip bow saw. Rip saws are used to cut along the length of the grain. If the blade of such a bow saw could not be turned, it could cut only a few inches before the stretcher would hit the end of the board being ripped.

Turnbuckle on the left, toggle on the right. (Below) Morticing the stretcher.

Two turning saws and a crosscut.

It's an easy arrangement to make. You bore holes through the bottoms of the two uprights and fashion two knobs with slotted shafts to fit through them. The end of the blade is held in the slot by an iron pin that passes through both the shaft and the hole in the blade. On smaller saws you may want to make the knob and shaft in two parts, the shaft a threaded metal rod that screws into the wooden knob. Larger saws can use one-piece knobs of a suitably tough material, such as dogwood or hornbeam.

The best-looking and longest lasting cord is the heavy waxed linen thread used for stitching leather. Wrap ten or so turns around the horns of the uprights, leaving enough free at each end to spiral around and through the multistranded cables thus formed. Place the toggle stick through the space in the middle, wind it up, and you're ready to work.

Frame Saws

While the bow saw uses the twisted cord to tighten the blade, a frame saw uses the blade itself to hold the works together. By spanning the blade between the ends of a wooden rectangle, it can be strained with wedges or a wing nut arrangement. Since the

Making Bow Saw Webs

The obvious source of webs is the local shop or dealer that has short lengths of band saw blades for discard or sale. These are readily available in many widths and gauges, but the teeth on them are rarely satisfactory for handwork. The answer is to grind, file, or snap off the old teeth and cut in new ones. Put the blade upright in a sharpening clamp and file-joint it straight down its length where the old teeth were. Starting on the left end, file in the tooth shape (rip or crosscut) that you want. It takes but a few seconds. Move over what appears to be an appropriate distance and do the next one and so on down the blade. You will be surprised how fast and accurately you can do this. Count the strokes of the file for each tooth if it helps you to do so. When the teeth are shaped, follow the sharpening procedure as outlined later.

The blade will usually be easy to file once you get past the old teeth, which may be very hard. If the ends of the blade are too hard to drill through for the pin holes to hold the web in the frame, heat them until they turn blue and let them cool and they will soften up.

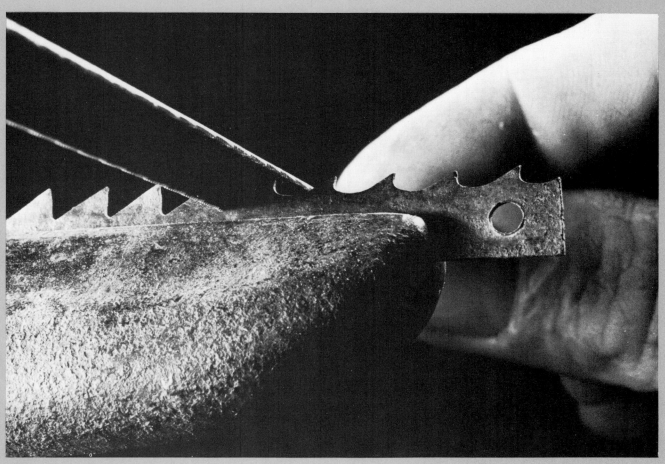

Filing rip teeth into an old band-saw blade.

This frame saw is odd in that the stretchers are morticed to take the end pieces.

blade is in the middle rather than on the side of the rectangle, this saw works well for ripping timbers; the frame passes on either side of the wood. The most common frame saw is the wheelwright's felly saw, which he uses to cut the arcing segments of the rim of the wheel. Rarer are saws used for cutting veneer from a log and framed "pit" saws used for sawing out planks.

Frame saws are also easy to make. The critical element of the design is the correct orientation of the joints in the frame. The two stretchers parallel to the blade are tenoned on their ends and the end pieces morticed to receive them.

Backsaws

Another means of strengthening the blade mimics the ancient design in which the teeth were set into a rigid back. The thick stiffener of a backsaw reduces the depth to which the blade can cut, but since such saws are primarily used in joinery, this is not a problem.

Backsaws are often known by the particular joint they are intended to cut. The smallest and finest are dovetail saws, fine toothed and often with no set at all in the teeth. Next come tenon saws in graduated sizes (sash, carcase, and so forth), which are used to cut both the shoulders and cheeks of these joints. Finally, there are long backsaws intended for use with miter boxes.

One form of the backsaw takes additional advantage of the stiffening back to use it as a depth stop. This is the staircase saw, used to cut the housings in the stringers to take the treads and risers. The wooden back of the staircase saw has two protrusions to use for handles. The exposure of the blade is adjustable by means of screws passing through the wooden stock into slots in the blade. To use a staircase saw set the blade exposure to the desired depth, saw the sides of the housing until it bottoms out, and then remove the waste with a chisel.

The staircase saw is about the only backsaw likely to be made by the user. Metal-backed saws are precision instruments often reflecting the height of the saw maker's art. Sometimes you will encounter a metal-backed saw that shows a distinct warping in the blade caused by its being carelessly twisted as the saw was used. This can occasionally be corrected by gently striking the back edge of the saw down on a flat surface to force the blade to reseat itself in the back. It's a somewhat frightening operation to undertake because you can easily do more harm than good.

The imprint on the back of my favorite saw reads: "R. Groves & Sons—Beehive Works—Sheffield—Cast Steel—Elastic Spring Temper—Warranted Good."

Handsaws

The first question many ask about old broad-bladed handsaws is, "What's this little nib for?" They're not on the handsaws that one sees today, but steel handsaws made before the mid-twentieth century commonly had a tiny protrusion, a "nib," near the toe end of the blade of the saw. You will hear all sorts of explanations—that it's an aid to starting the cut, that it's used for securing a wooden blade guard, or even that it's to keep the saw from sliding out of the carpenter's tool basket.

Practical men want to see a practical use for all things, but the origin of the nib is probably a decorative one—a vestige of the decorative filigree work found on the early Dutch and Swedish handsaws. It's something akin to the pathetic chrome strip found on the front fenders of Buicks where the once-proud Cruiserline Vent-i-ports formerly reigned.

Good handsaws are taper ground:

The staircase saw.

Crosscut versus Rip

Think of wood as a bundle of fibers all glued together, because that is what it is. Now consider how you would go about neatly severing these fibers to make slots first across their length (crosscutting) and then along their length (ripping).

In crosscutting, the wood and the saw behave like that sheaf of wheat being severed by the series of flint knives. The knives, precisely oriented and angled on a crosscutting saw, cleanly slice across the fibers on both extremities of the width of the kerf and carry the dust out in the gullets. The leading edge of each tooth is tilted forward to slice the outer surface before the deeper part of the cut is made, just as you would instinctively angle a pocketknife to make a similar cut.

Now turn your mind to cutting this bundle along its length. Imagine that you try to do it with the same saw that works so well for crosscutting. Instead of slicing the fibers, the teeth now ride along and on either side of them. To effectively cut this bundle of fibers along their length, you need to attack them with a series of chisels, not with knives. A rip saw is simply this, a series of chisels oriented so that they continually chop off the ends of the fibers as you work.

Crosscut teeth are like knives; rip teeth are like chisels.

Cutting across the grain.

Ripping along the grain.

that is, the metal is thinner on the back than it is on the tooth side to permit an easier passage through the kerf. It may also be ground thinner near the toe end of the back than it is at the handle end. The precision of this grinding and the homogeneity of the steel and its temper can be tested by bending the blade in your hands. The evenness of the bend, the stiffness of the return to the flat, and the tone of the blade when struck with the thumb will give you an indication of the quality of the steel. At the very least, you will make a good showing with the person you're buying the saw from.

Be wary of an old saw that seems to have a permanent kink, a warp, or, even worse, a buckle in it. Sometimes you can flex out a bend, but a buckle —a high spot that shows as a shiny place in the middle of the blade—can be stretched out only by hand hammering on the metal around the damaged spot. It can be done, but it's not at all easy. I have often heard that you can flatten a bent saw by bringing it down in a sharp slap on a calm pool of water. I have either not been striking hard enough or was expecting too much because all I accomplished was getting myself soaking wet and upsetting the bull frogs.

As long as a blade is in good shape, it really doesn't matter what sort of teeth a saw has on it, rip or crosscut, fine or coarse, because you can file or grind away the old ones and replace them with what you want. A saw shop can do it for you or you can do it yourself. Rip saws straight from the factory are generally made longer, from 28 to 30 inches; crosscuts range from 14 to 26 inches.

Starting a rip cut with a handsaw bearing a stout nib.

The tone tells all.

One of various overhand grips for ripping.

Sawing

Starting the saw at the beginning of a cut can give some people a fit. Assuming you are right handed, hold your left hand around the end of the wood and place your left thumb against the toe of the blade of the saw to hold it steady. Draw the blade lightly back and forth and the cut will begin. Lightly is the key. Saws can be cut with finer teeth at the toe end of the blade to make this go easier.

As Joseph Moxon put it in 1673, "The Excellency of Sawing is, to keep the Kerf exactly in the line marked out to be sawn, without wriggling on either, or both sides." Once the cut is started, the saw is generally inclined at a 45-degree angle to the surface for crosscutting and a 60-degree angle for ripping. Depending on what you are out to accomplish, you may want to saw right on the line, saw down its side, or split the line with the edge of

the kerf. The condition of the teeth has everything to do with how easily and accurately you are able to manage this. A saw that constantly bears to one side or binds in the kerf needs attention.

Don't try to twist the saw along its long axis to correct a misdirected cut. Rather, hold it at a more acute angle to the work surface and bend it slightly along its length to make the kerf lead in the right direction. When crosscutting thick rectangular stock, it's best to saw diagonally into the corner first and then bring the saw around square to finish the job. This way you can be sure of getting a truly square cut.

There is a peculiar way of ripping boards with the saw held backwards in an overhand grip. This is a common practice in cabinet shops because the high work benches, which do so well for crosscutting and planing, are too high to allow the saw to be conveniently used in the normal manner.

There's nothing slow about this way of working. Sharp tools and experience can do wonderful things.

Two-Man Crosscuts

We know a good deal about crosscut saws from the medieval period from representations of St. Simon the Apostle, who was martyred by being sawn in half. Tradition has it that he was sawn in half lengthwise, but he is, nonetheless, typically shown holding a crosscut saw.

Two-man crosscut saws are, in the interest of fairness and efficiency, designed to cut in both directions. The standard tooth pattern of a handsaw is most efficient in only one direction because the leading edge of each tooth is canted to form a more obtuse angle to the fibers of the wood. Of course, this is not possible in a saw that must cut equally well in both directions. An equilateral tooth, moreover, 60 degrees on both faces, "lays down" more on the work and will not cut as deeply or remove sawdust as efficiently as a steeper face.

There are two ways around this problem. The first is to keep the teeth symmetrical, but make them longer and sharper. This increases the angle of the cutting face on both sides of the tooth, but such a saw is more easily dulled by cutting hard woods. The second approach, sketched by Leonardo but dating from earlier in the fifteenth century, is the addition of cutting surfaces at right angles to the wood. In the earliest pattern, the teeth are set in pairs shaped like a series of M's. The vertical sides of the M (it is upside down when in contact with the wood) act as "rakers" to push out the fibers severed by the two internal slicing surfaces. Later patterns add additional slicing teeth within the M, the U-shaped gullets between the oppos-

Sharpening Raker-Tooth Crosscuts

Saws for cutting in both directions will often have "raker" teeth to clean out the bottom of the kerf after the grain has been severed on either side by the regular crosscutting teeth. Sharpen these saws by first jointing the teeth by lightly pulling a file along them, taking care to hold the file exactly square to the sides of the blade. Brighten the tips of all the slicing teeth, but don't worry about the rakers. The rakers are intended to be recessed below the other teeth, so you don't have to touch them as yet. File the profile of the slicing teeth to a 60-degree point and the bevels at 45 degrees until the flats from jointing disappear. The rakers are filed at right angles to the blade and the line of the teeth, just like rip teeth. There are special files called "cant saw" files available to match the angle of the valley between the raker pairs. File the rakers until they sit about the thickness of a worn dime below the points of the other teeth.

Lance-tooth teeth are easy to set. You take the file and set the tang end between two teeth and turn the file to the side to bend the pair in opposite directions. One third the thickness of the blade is the maximum a tooth should be bent out. The rakers are left square in line with the blade. When all is right, the saw works easy and pulls out long strings of wood, severed by the slicers and planed free by the rakers.

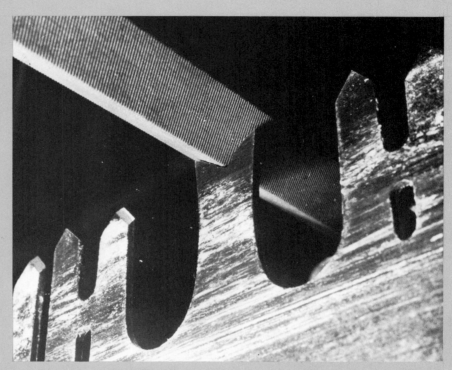

File the rakers with a cant saw file.

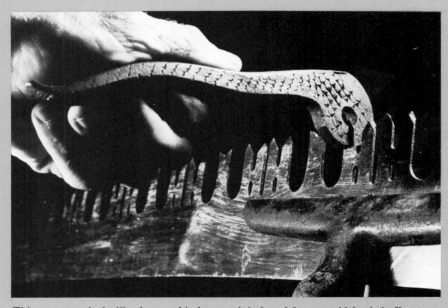

This saw wrest looks like dragon skin because it is forged from an old farrier's file.

Congenial company makes pleasant work.

ing raker faces occurring at every third or fourth tooth. Finally, the "lance-tooth" pattern places the rakers and the slicing teeth on long pedestals that make sharpening easy.

A further refinement of this tooth pattern is the addition of a web of steel linking the extended slicing teeth at the midpoint of their pedestals. This web strengthens the teeth but still allows for easy sharpening, as the file cuts right through them to the base of the gullets. This last pattern is called the "perforated lance tooth" from the appearance of the holes beneath the strengthening web.

Crosscutting

It is only within the last century that the crosscut saw has replaced the axe in felling timber. Crosscut saws were found in the carpenter's yard but not in the forest, not at least until the tree was down on the ground. Even so, the wide opening cut on the falling side is best made with the axe, the back cut alone being made with the saw.

One of the primary skills of using a two-man crosscut saw is that of adroitly insulting your co-worker with the object of motivating him or her to ease your labors. The basic invective is "Quit ridin' the saw!"—delivered to a partner who seems to be resisting your pull stroke. "Pick up your feet!" is a more advanced calumny, implying that you are resigned to the burden of your partner's riding the saw as long as he doesn't drag his feet as he does so. A grumbled "Quit wrappin' the saw around your leg!" will suggest to your partner that you think he's being somewhat inattentive in keeping the saw in line with the kerf.

Beyond a proficiency in hyperbolic derision, a crosscut sawyer must develop a light and rhythmic touch. You don't want to bear down into the cut, but rather pull the saw across the surface and "let the saw do the work." The blade of the saw is designed in a convex arc to match the swing of your arms. You're not supposed to push a crosscut saw, only pull. Pushing a long "misery whip" is akin to pushing a rope. Too hard a push will indeed cause the saw to bend in the kerf and drag, but experienced sawyers can add just enough pressure to feed the saw back and help matters along considerably.

Bucking a tree into log lengths can be torment when the kerf keeps pinching the saw. This is particularly troublesome when a tree lands so that it is supported only at the ends. You get halfway through and suddenly find the saw seized by several tons of pressure. The best way around this is

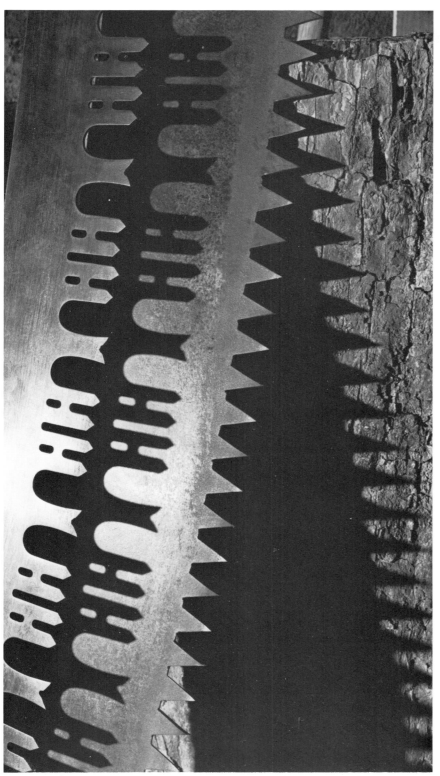

Perforated lance tooth on the left and peg tooth on the right.

to use a little foresight and arrange the landing spot so that the tree will be supported in the middle rather than on the ends. The support needs to be a cushion of brush or rotten logs so that the shock of landing will not cause damage to the tree.

Lacking such foresight or luck, you can drive wedges into the kerf above the saw to keep it open. If you wait too long to do this, though, wedging will have no effect at all. You may then find it necessary to lever the log up and place a support beneath it or to roll the log halfway over and continue the cut from the side. If you don't have a cant hook handy, be sure to leave one long limb on the log to use as a lever to aid in this rolling.

If none of this works (and assuming you can get the saw free from the kerf), you may well want to make a second saw kerf parallel to and an inch or so over from the first. When this kerf starts to pinch, pull the saw out and, standing on top of the log, swing down with the poll of your axe and pop out the intervening wood. Now set a big wedge in the top of the wide kerf and continue sawing on down.

The occasional application of kerosene to the blade of the saw and alcohol to the gullets of the sawyers makes the work go smoother.

Sharpening Saws

To sharpen a saw you need both knowledge and character. Not only do you have to understand how the teeth function in the wood but you must maintain a disciplined, systematic consistency throughout the whole process. There are four steps in sharpening a saw: jointing, shaping, setting, and sharpening.

Jointing is the process of making sure that all the teeth are at the same height. Clamp the saw, teeth up, be-

Jointing a bucksaw web.

Shaping crosscut teeth.

tween boards in a vise or in a special saw-sharpening clamp. Take a fine flat file and lightly drag it square along the length of the teeth at dead right angles to the side of the blade. You must hold the file at a precise right angle to the blade or you will be making the teeth higher on one side of the blade than on the other. Such an error will cause the saw to pull to one side, just as the mountain cattle of yore with longer legs on their downhill side could only walk in circles when they got on flat land. Joint lightly and precisely until you brighten the tips of all the teeth. One or two passes should be enough for saws without broken teeth.

Finer saw teeth call for smaller files. Coarser-toothed saws with four to eight points to the inch need a 6-inch slim taper file. Those with nine to ten points need an extra slim, and a double extra slim file will be required for saws with eleven to twelve points. Even more finely toothed saws will need a 5-inch superfine file.

Shaping, the next step, puts the teeth at their appropriate profile for their alloted task. Both crosscut and rip teeth are shaped with the same equilaterally triangular file called a "slim taper." The 60-degree angles of the corners of this file can cut both shapes of teeth, the difference being made by the axial tilt given to the file as the teeth are cut.

Rip teeth are filed so that their cutting face is at 90 degrees to the line of the tops of the teeth. Thus, if the handle of the saw were to your left as you were filing, you would shape the teeth with the left face of the triangular file held vertically. Crosscutting teeth, however, are shaped with a 12-to-15-degree slope off the vertical on their faces and the file must be held accordingly.

Shape the teeth by filing straight across without dipping the file on either side. Start at one end on the face of a tooth that leans away from

Shaping rip teeth.

Setting back saw teeth with a wrest.

you and file it and the back of the adjacent tooth until you reach the middle of the flats caused by jointing. Skip to the next gullet where the face of the tooth leans away from you and do the same thing. Work your way down the length of the saw, doing every other gullet and then reverse the saw in the vise and repeat the process down the other side. On this second run, the filing should take off the remaining half of the jointing flat, and the teeth will all be sharply pointed and equal in depth, height, and angle.

Once the teeth are all the proper size and shape they can be accurately set. Setting the teeth means bending them slightly to alternate sides, right and left in turn. The set gives the blade clearance in the kerf and makes a great difference in how the saw performs. Never try to reverse the directions of the set on an old saw. There is no point to it, and you are likely to break off a lot of teeth. The maximum amount of set to put into any given tooth is to have it lean one-third of the thickness of the blade to the side, bent at a point halfway down from the tip. You may want this maximum amount for coarse cutting in green wood and considerably less (or none) for dry. You can always add more set if you don't have enough.

There are numerous devices for setting saws, some easier to use than others. The saw "wrest" is a wrench-like slotted bar used to twist adjacent pairs of teeth in alternate directions. By setting the slot on the tops of two teeth and turning the handle to the side, you bend one in one direction, the other in the other direction. You work your way down the length of the saw, two teeth at a time.

Patent pistol lever saw sets are perhaps the easiest to use, as well as the easiest to overset the saw with. If you don't have the instructions that came with such a set, experiment on your saw at the handle end, starting

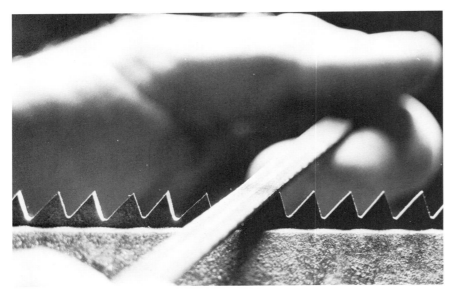

Sharpening crosscut teeth.

Time spent in sharpening is seldom wasted. An hour of patience in sharpening saves many hours of impatience at work. It's an exacting process but one that you can learn. You'll often hear of how saw sharpening was a secret art, the practitioner working behind closed doors, ringing a bell to let the customer know to come in when the job was done. It may well be that the technique was considered a professional secret by some and closely guarded. But just try to sharpen a saw with someone looking over your shoulder; you'll end up locking the doors too.

with what appears to be the minimum adjustment. Set the teeth from both sides or you won't be able to tell what the total effect will be. The set must be equal on both sides of the saw or it will tend to pull to the side in a most infuriating manner as you work.

You can also set saw teeth by setting them over an anvil stake and hitting them with a hammer. This is hardly done any more (and I have never tried it).

Sharpening now puts the edge on the teeth. For crosscutting teeth, work as in shaping with the file on the face of a tooth that leans away from you, except now angle the handle of the file back at 45 degrees toward the handle of the saw. Don't dip too much, just angle back. File the face of the one tooth and the back of the adjacent tooth simultaneously until you form half of the point on each of them. Do

every other pair down one side of the saw and then flip the saw around and do the remaining teeth. As a final measure on crosscuts, you may wish to lightly pass a whetstone flat down both sides of the blade to ease the burrs and give an even, polished cut.

After being set, rip teeth are no longer properly oriented to work as well as they should. Both their tops and faces should be at right angles to the blade and the line of the teeth. Bending the teeth to the sides cants the angles of the tops and twisting the teeth cants the angles of the faces. Depending on how you set the teeth, these aspects now need to be corrected. Usually you will need one more light jointing pass and then two light shaping passes from opposite sides of the saw to bring the teeth to sharpness at their proper 90-degree angle.

THE WHETSTONE QUARRY

His axes schall I make fulle scharpe,
That thei may lyghtly do ther werke
To make my master a ryche man
I schall asey, if that I canne.

"The Debate of the Carpenter's Tools" (fifteenth century)

We made our first serious attempt to locate the old whetstone quarry on a day so hot you'd break a sweat just buttering your cornbread. We made several stops along the road where it should have been, but no one we spoke to had seen anything that looked like a mine or quarry. One man said that he had encountered some deep holes off to the west while hunting, but our triangulations on a modern map placed the quarry to the east, so we decided to head on up the ridge and have a look about.

We walked up a cleared right-of-way through the trees, where horses had gone before. There were patches of poison ivy all about, and the occasional kamikaze deer fly went berserk in the presence of its first victim of the season. As we neared a second ridge, the deer flies broke off their attack, and I could see on the crest boulders about the size of bushel baskets that had been exposed in cutting through the narrow right-of-way.

The big rocks looked promising, but only slowly did the old workings begin to reveal themselves. I first spotted the remains of an old road intersecting the path. It was all but paved solid with angular, blue-grey stone rubble. We pushed through the arched brush over the old path, and immediately to our left we could see about a quarter acre of rubble of all sizes partially covered with leaf humus. The rock was fine and dark, and I went excitedly from rock to rock, handing them to Tom. "Try this one," I'd say. He would take it in his hand, test it between his fingers, and proclaim it "greasy," as though this were the highest level attainable in the mineral kingdom. We stopped our excavations long enough to make a quick foray down the old ridge road in either direction to assure ourselves that this was indeed the main workings. Apparently, this rubble pile on the ridge was it.

Looking for the good stuff.

Follow the natural cleavage.

After an hour or so of picking and digging, we collected an armload each of smooth flat rocks and made our way back into town, busily honing our pocketknives as we went. We both ran out of spit well before the first mile, and the stones were thoroughly glazed.

Back at the shop I took one of the likelier-looking stones and began to dress it. After about ten minutes of rubbing on the side of a broken sandstone wheel kept constantly flushed with water, the surface shone like deep green marble. Giving the rock a splash of kerosene, I gave it a proper trial on a chisel. It was as good a stone as I had ever used.

Of course my opinion is probably prejudiced by the adventure of having found the old quarry on the ridge, for this kind of rediscovery is one of my favorite events. Even if the stones had not been that good, they would have been priceless to me.

I decided to find out more about this quarry on the hill. For years it had been just an annoying enigma for me on the tattered 1891 map of the county that hung on the back wall of the shop. I asked several of the old families in the surrounding area if they had ever heard of the quarry. Finally, I found one woman who remembered her father's mentioning the old whetstone mine. She had never seen it, though, and I promised her that we would make a trip up there so that she could.

Finding only hints of information from the local people, I contacted the geology department at the local university. Only seven miles distant from the quarry and having had a school of mineralogy since 1820, it figured to have some record of it somewhere.

Within a few days a professor there had managed to locate a report published in the American Journal of Science for 1828 on the geology of North Carolina written by Dennis Olmstead, who was himself a professor of chem-

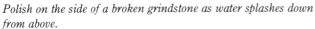

Polish on the side of a broken grindstone as water splashes down from above.

The translucent edge of McCauley stones.

istry and mineralogy at the university. This report provided a goldmine of information.

"The most valuable bed that I have met with," he said, "is about seven miles west of Chapel-Hill. It is known by the name of M'Cauley's quarry. It has been opened on the summit of hill, which forms one of three parallel ranges extending from north east to south west." This is exactly where we had been 160 years later. The overgrown ridge road passing by it was apparently well traveled then because he went on to say that "although many thousand hones have been taken from this spot by travellers and others, yet as the quarry has not been wrought for the market, the excavations have been carried to very little depth."

Olmstead found great variations in quality among stones obtained from the same spot, describing the best as having an olive green color and transparent edges. The best were apparently very good, as he goes on to say. "Our carpenters lay aside, for them, the best Turkey hones of the market. . . . Some of the specimens, when polished, present a clouded or chequered surface, with a high lustre, and possess no small degree of beauty. Mechanics, in the vicinity of the quarry, frequently supply themselves with masses of eight or ten pounds weight. One side being faced, it is used as a hone, and is generally valued in proportion to the time it has been in use, for thus it acquires smoothness and hardness. The quality is frequently much improved by be-

coming thoroughly soaked with oil."

So the stones were important and, according to my source at the university, about 600 million years old. They were probably formed from fine volcanic ash that settled in this spot when it was an archipelago in a primordial sea, as Indonesia is today. Heat and pressure slowly compressed the volcanic debris into the beds of "slate" that now cap this ridge in the woods.

Beginnings

It wasn't long after man began to use rocks for tools that he noticed their abrasive qualities and put them to use for polishing first other stones and

Other Places

This guide to the locations of potential whetstone sources is adapted from a list published in the *Annual Report of the Geological Survey of Arkansas for 1890*, volume 3, *Whetstones and Novaculites of Arkansas*, by L. S. Griswold. I have not attempted to correct any of the misspellings of the locations given here for fear of doing more harm than good. Your state geology department should have more detailed records for your own area. Good hunting!

Alabama
Sandstone is quarried near Eldridge, in Walker County.

Arkansas
"A quarry of this mineral [novaculite], three miles above the Hot Springs of Washitaw, has often been noticed by travelers for its extent and excellency of its quality" (Henry R. Schoolcraft, 1819). Lower Silurian novaculite is found in the following counties: Garland, Hot Spring, Howard, Montgomery, Pike, Polk, Pulaski, and Saline.

Dakota
Sandstone is found near Buffalo Gap in Custer County and schist near Tigerville in Pennington County.

Georgia
There is novaculite in Lincoln County on a low hill two miles from the Lincolnton courthouse, projecting nearly vertically from the ground over an area of four or five acres. It is straw-colored to greenish white. It is also found near Graves Mountain. Another whetstone grit is found in McDuffie, Heard, Troup, Oglethorpe, and Meriweather counties.

Indiana
Hindostan quarries were opened about 1840. Two stones are quarried, one a shoemaker's sandstone and the other a very fine grained, compact sandstone, used chiefly for whetstones by carpenters, mechanics, and others. These are found in Orange County, French Licks 9, and Orangeville 2.

Maine
Novaculite is found in abundance near the forks of the Kennebec, eighty or ninety miles from Hallowell. Silurian novaculite is found near Phillips and Temple in Franklin County. There is Huronian serpentine novaculite on Little Deer Island and Western Island in Hancock County. Sandstone may be found at Nutter's Head in Washington County and Cambrian novaculite at York in York County.

Maryland
Cambrian novaculite is found on the Patuxent River, near the road to Washington. Anne Arundle or Prince George counties.

Massachusetts
The vicinity of Boston furnishes compact feldspar analogous to the Turkey stone. This lower Silurian novaculite slate of Middlesex County is found near Cambridge, Charlestown, Concord, and Malden. In Bellingham, 22,800 mica schist whetstones were manufactured in 1838. In Essex County, Silurian novaculite is found near Nahant. Lower Silurian mica schist was worked commercially prior to 1841 at Enfield, Norwich, and Cummington in Hampshire County. Other novaculite slates are found in Norfolk County at Dedham, Milton, and Quincy and in Suffolk County at Brighton, Brookline, and Dorchester.

Michigan
Huronian novaculite slate is found at Carp River and Teal Lake in Ontonagon County and at L'Anse in Baraga County. Sandstone is found in many places in Huron County.

Mississippi
There is good sandstone on Big Bear Creek in Tishamingo County.

Missouri
Sandstone is found in many places in Randolph and Barton counties, at Pierce City in Lawrence County, and at O'Bannon's quarry in Madison County.

New Hampshire
A fine-grained stone from Lisbon in Grafton County was known as the "chocolate." Those from Orford came from the shore of Indian Pond and were sold under the "Indian Pond" brand name. Other Grafton County stones are found at Littleton, Haverill, and Piermont. A Silurian novaculite is found at Tamworth in Carroll County.

New York
There is Silurian and Cambrian novaculite slate in Columbia County at Clermont, Germantown, Greenport, Livingstone, Rogers Island, Stockport, and Stuyvesant. There is sandstone at Labrador Lake in Cortland County and Beaver Kill River and Monticello in Delaware County. Silurian whetslates are found in Rensselaer County.

North Carolina

The stones from McPherson's quarry in Chatham County, five miles west of Woodin's ferry on the Haw River, havè a finer and softer grit than McCauley's. They are bluish and yellowish white. On the Salisbury Road in Randolph County, near Deep River, is a bed of a similar kind, highly valued by the inhabitants. Other fine stones are found at Barbee's mill, two miles south of Chapel Hill, on the Flat River in the eastern part of Person County to the narrows of the Neuse, and near Wadesboro in Anson County.

Ohio

Sandstones are found at Berea in Cuyahoga County, Amherst in Lorain County, Hocking River in Hocking County, Manchester in Summit County, and Farmington and Mesopotamia in Trumbull County.

Pennsylvania

Lower Silurian sandstone is found in Berks County at Oley. Cambrian micaceous sandstone is in Delaware County at Avondale, Darby Creek, Marple, Township 2, Springfield, and east of Swarthmore. Cambrian mica schist is in Chester County at Hayes's quarry on the Newlin Township line and in the middle of the county.

Rhode Island

The Geology of Rhode Island in 1840 reported production in Smithfield of six to eight thousand dozens of whetstones. Mica schist is found one-half mile northeast of Woonsocket village, extending a mile southwest.

South Carolina

Huronian novaculite is found in Abbeville and Edgefield counties and on Turkey Creek in Chester County.

Tennessee

There is sandstone near Knoxville and on the French Broad River a mile above Dandridge in Jefferson County.

Vermont

There are oilstone quarries on an island in Lake Memphremagog. The island is about seven miles west of Stanstead Village. One quarry is now entirely underwater and the other partly so. These were large quarries with stones of good repute. There is Cambrian novaculite slate at Thetford in Orange County and at Guilford and Marlborough in Windham County. Huronian mica schist is in Windsor County at Ludlow, Plymouth, and Stockbridge. Cambrian mica schist is found in Newport, Trasburg, and Brownington. There is Huronian talcose schist at Northfield in Washington County and mica schist at Berkshire and Fairfield in Franklin County.

then the newfangled tools of bronze and iron.

A wide variety of natural materials have been used to grind and polish metal. The natural stones are usually known by the name of their source. Beyond the familiar Arkansas stone, there are the Turkey stone, the Belgian, the Labrador, the Naxian, the Tam O' Shanter, the Washita, the Charnley Forest, and the Water of Ayr, among countless others. The Arkansas and the Washita are among those known to mineralogists today as novaculites, from the Latin word *novacula*, meaning "a razor." Another good word is the Celtic name for whetstone, *passernix*.

Other materials have been used as well. Britons once sharpened their scythes on wooden "ripe sticks" covered with tallow and sand. Armorers polished metal with handfuls of "scouring rushes" or "horse tails," a plant which isolates silica in its cells. For stropping, leather, often charged with jewelers rouge (available at hardware stores as buffing compound), is the most commonly used material. I have occasionally used the undersides of woody shelf fungi that grow out of the sides of trees for this purpose.

The makers of artificial stones try to capture some of the romance of natural materials by giving them such names as the "India," but they are made of bonded synthetic abrasives such as silicon carbide. In his *Dictionary of Tools*, R. A. Salaman relates the story of a Brixton ironmonger who, when he could not convince carpenters of the value of the new artificial oil stones (this was in 1901), would throw one against the wall. As the stone would not break, he sometimes made the sale. These artificial stones have largely replaced the natural ones in today's market, except for the finest work.

The favored natural abrasive was, and is, about the most common material on earth, silicon dioxide, silica—

They're a lot easier to use if you take them off the tree.

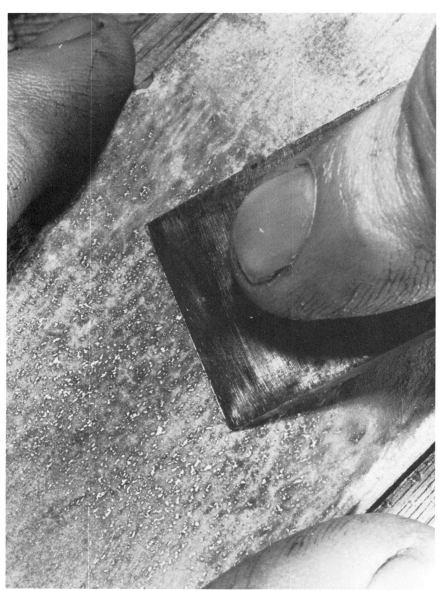

This stone has glazed because the metal has worn away faster than the stone.

sand. Indeed, the root of the word *sand* goes back to the ancient Greek *psēn*, meaning "to rub." Silica is hard and sharp when the grains are fresh. When rubbed about, though, the sharp edges become rounded and will no longer cut as well. Beach sand, which has been knocked about a lot, will not work as well as grit that is freshly eroded from the rock. In his report on McCauley's whetstones, Olmstead mentioned that one of their desirable qualities was that they "wear away fast." Using such a stone constantly reveals fresh surfaces of sharp particles. A stone that does not wear away faster than the metal that it is abrading will quickly glaze and stop cutting, either from the sharp edges having been rounded or from the particles of metal filling the spaces between the abrasive grains.

The oil for honing that Olmstead mentioned helps to prevent this last problem by holding the metal particles in suspension and keeping the grit clean. The suspended particles of grit also aid in polishing the edge. The water that is used on sandstones for grinding also washes away worn par-

ticles and softens the surface of the stone so that it will wear more readily.

Olmstead said that the McCauley stones will "set a fine edge" because "their grit is both fine and sharp." The size of the grit determines how finely the metal surface will be worked by contact with the stone. Abrasive stones work by scratching away the metal surface. When you grind a chisel on a sandstone wheel, the large particles take deep, widely spaced

scratches out of the surface. This quickly shapes the metal, but leaves the edge too rough and ragged to part the fibers of the wood cleanly. When you then hone this edge on a stone with smaller particles, the scratches produced are shallower and closer together. The result is a polished edge that is finer and keener, and one that will meet with less resistance as it is forced through the bundles of cellulose that we call wood.

The sandstone must be kept constantly flushed with water when in use. If allowed to stand in water, however, it will be permanently softened and wear unevenly.

The finest stones are those that have the smallest grain size and the least amount of foreign matter between the abrasive particles of the rock. The highly regarded Arkansas stones can be almost pure silica and appear pure white. Foreign matter colors stones and affects their cutting action by dispersing the actively abrasive grains so that the scratches they make are further apart. These impurities can cause a great variation in

how the stone will wear, faster or slower, and will determine in large part the tendency of the stone to glaze.

Carpenters generally prefer a soft, fast-wearing stone, both because it cuts quickly and because the broad blades of carpenter's tools will wear away the stone evenly across its surface. The best way to obtain a final edge on a soft or porous stone is to draw the blade backward across its

face. I usually do this for a few strokes after I work the edge in a circular motion on the whole surface of the stone.

The narrow tools of carvers would quickly gouge out the soft stones that carpenters and joiners usually use. They must have as hard a stone as possible to resist irregular wear. The hard black Arkansas is their stone of choice.

Care of Stones

All whetstones need to be kept in a wooden box to protect them from breakage, dirt, and the elements. A stone that is exposed to the sun will harden and tend to glaze. Clean your stone with plenty of oil or water after each use and put it away. The wooden box will retain some of the oil or water and keep the stone fresh for its next use.

Protect the surface of the stone by working the tool being sharpened over the whole of its width, not just to one side. Inevitably, the ends of the stone will get to be higher than the middle. When this gets to be a nuisance, you can resurface the stone by rubbing it against another one (a chunk of sandstone is excellent) or on a sheet of abrasive paper set on a flat surface.

In many of the old towns of Europe the stone step of the stairway of a certain house was discovered incidentally to be a good whetstone. This spot would eventually become community property and be worn slowly away under countless kitchen knives. Chances are there is some worthy stone near you just waiting to go to work. If you cut your own trees, why not your own rock?

The surface left by the sandstone.

The finer scratches left by a Belgian hone.

A century-old white Arkansas stone in its case. It will leave the metal with a mirror finish.

CROW CHASERS AND TURKEY CALLS

They are great Enemies to the Corn Fields.

John Lawson, *A New Voyage to Carolina* (1708)

A war surplus gas alarm.

Defenders of the farm, hickory-throated, ratchet-slapping crow chasers counterattack black flocks in the cornfield. Too awful to lie quiet the year out, these rowdies crack the night of the New Year. They once called constabulary to the crime, sailors to the fight, and, more recently, soldiers and civilians to prepare for an attack by poison gas. The first of these that I ever made was lost in a keg of ale in back of some dark tavern in the final hours of a Halloween night, along with a pitchfork, a monkey mask, and my reputation. Coarse engines they may be, but they are quick and interesting to make—and useful too: they will instantly explode the grackles from the largest of cherry trees.

The crow chaser I show here is made, as it should be, from scraps, the four parts of four different woods. The handle shaft is walnut; the arm, beech; the ratchet gear, dogwood; and the reed, hickory. Making it involves thinking that is also salvaged, useful bits from the scrap bin of serious endeavor.

The Handle

Make the handle first, turned long and fat enough to fill your fist and with a shaft about as long as your finger and thicker than a pencil, matching the size of one of your auger bits. The midsection of the shaft, where the gear will be fixed, should be left full sized so that the bored gear will fit tightly on it. The places above and below this midsection where the arm holding the reed will ride should be

turned a hair undersized so that the arm will swing freely. Remove the completed handle from the lathe, but leave the places on the ends where the lathe centers were fitted undisturbed. You will need to use them again later.

The Ratchet Gear

My gear is made from a half-seasoned, 1¼-inch-long piece of dogwood cut off a branch as a whole disk. Dogwood is tough and has unusual resistance to the splitting and checking caused by the differential shrinkage of a whole stem section, but it would probably still split were it not for the hole that you will bore right through the center of this disk. Like the preboring of the

Bore the dogwood ratchet blank.

wheelwright's elm hub, this hole gives the shrinkage of the piece somewhere to go. Your dogwood shouldn't be green as a gourd, but neither should it have begun to develop cracks already. If you don't have dogwood, the toughest wood you can find will do.

Bore the shaft hole through the center as square to the two sawn faces as you can manage. Now take the piece and jam it onto the handle shaft. Return this assemblage to the lathe and turn the gear true to the shaft, about 2 inches in diameter. Turn the two sawn faces true, leaving a little shoulder all the way around about a half inch in from the edge. This shoulder will be a guide to tell you how deep to cut the teeth in the gear, which is the next step.

Pull the gear off the shaft and set it in the vise so that the jaws of the vise are on the end grain. Using any saw that's handy, cut the sides of the first gear space down to the turned shoulder and snap out the intervening wood. Your saw cuts must be angled enough to give the root of the teeth sufficient strength. If a tooth looks weak, it is weak and will probably break out, leaving a gap and producing a "crack!-crack!-crack!-thud!" effect. You could try and space off the teeth with dividers, but you can do just as well by cutting right-looking teeth one after the other and then fudging on the last three teeth as you close the circle.

The Arm

Find or cut a block of beech or other strong wood about 1½ inches thick, 3 inches wide, and 7 inches long. First bore the hole for the shaft through its width. This needs to be done before cutting the space for the reed, while the block is still solid. Otherwise, the passage of the auger through the narrow forks of the precut arm will cause them to split.

With the shaft hole bored, saw down the arm to create the sides of the space for the reed and gear, stopping 2 inches from the end. The width of this space must be just slightly greater than the thickness of the gear. Now using mallet and chisel, cut out the waste, going halfway through from one side and finishing up from the other. The reed itself is held by a narrow eighth-inch-wide slot cut along the width of the last 2 inches. Rather than saw first and finish with a chisel (you'd need too narrow a chisel), you first "stop" the slot with a gimlet hole and then finish with two saw cuts.

Turn the ratchet using the partially turned handle as a mandrel on the spring-pole lathe.

Saw stout teeth.

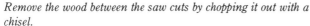

Remove the wood between the saw cuts by chopping it out with a chisel.

Saw down to the previously bored hole to make the slot for the reed.

The Reed

Put the gear in place in the arm and push the shaft of the handle through both. The arm should not bind on either the gear or the shaft. Split out a piece of hickory or ash or your local equivalent and shave it down to a stiff, tapering reed that will fit through the narrow slot of the arm and clear the sides of the large space. Test the response of the reed by turning the gear so as to make the appropriate racket, shaving to taste. When you arrive at a satisfactory dimension, saw off any excess and bore two offset gimlet holes through the arm and the reed. Shave pegs from bits of wood left from cutting the gear teeth and drive them into the holes. Another gimlet hole and peg through the gear and shaft to hold everything together and you're ready to raise corn or Cain as you see fit.

A Turkey Call

Terry, a friend from the valley in New Mexico where I lived, once shot a wild turkey's head off with a 30-30 rifle on Thanksgiving Day. He told me how he listened for them and watched for their tracks in the snow beneath the scrub oak and then waited for hours sitting in front of a tree. Wild turkeys can easily spot the slightest movement in the woods, but may not notice someone sitting directly in front of a tree. Apparently, they'll spot you every time if you try to peek around.

A while back I was in a friend's junk shop, looking at some used Bowler hats, when I spotted a small, handmade red cedar box. The box was carved from solid wood and had a cedar lid that was loosely fastened with a screw at one end and had an

The reed and gear are both held by pegs.

Edgar was not impressed.

extension to form a handle on the other. Partly out of curiosity and partly to avoid buying a too-small hat, I asked the owner what it was. She said that it was a turkey call and was just what I needed. I had never seen one before and I don't hunt, but as soon as I tried it, I had to have it. You work the thing by scissoring the lid quickly on the rim of one side of the box. If you do it just right, it sounds for all the world like a mechanical pelican in a hot argument with a Cambrian carter.

The call is not all that extraordinary in its construction. It's a hollowed-out block of heartwood red cedar measur-

ing 8½ inches long, 1¾ inches wide, and 2 inches deep. Looking inside, you can see that the hollowing was made by first boring a series of eight slightly overlapping one-inch-diameter holes and then cleaning out in between with a pocketknife. The side walls of the box had been carefully shaved so as to be quite thin at their upper edge where the lid makes contact but retain a full quarter inch thickness at the base. The lid, which is convex on its underside, was fastened to the box with a wood screw which had since pulled loose. I expect that earlier versions were secured with a leather thong, which would

have been a more durable solution. People have told me that there are many variations on this design and that tulip poplar is also used in making these calls.

You may not need a turkey call, but a box for that new whetstone might be in order. The process of hollowing out the box is the same for both, except that you must square the corners of the latter.

To hollow a box, you need moderately dry wood (be sure to whistle while you work if it's a turkey call you're making), an auger bit, and a chisel. You are less likely to split the sides of the box if you clamp the block

Remove the bulk of the wood with an auger.

in the jaws of a vise while you work.

I have always used common twist or center bits and spaced the holes with very little overlap so that they would not pull into the previously cut hole. You can usually get away with a bit more overlap if you bore two holes spaced a little over half the auger diameter apart and then bore out the web between them. An auger bit called a Forstner bit, which tracks on its periphery rather than just in its center, will allow you to take a more generous overlap. Such a bit also has a shallower centerpoint, reducing the chance that it will poke through on the far side of the wood as you work. They are a bit expensive, though, and you don't need one unless you plan to do a lot of this sort of work.

When you have bored all the holes, it's a simple matter to clean out the remaining waste wood with the chisel. Make the cross-grained cuts down the sides and ends with the flat side of the chisel held against the wood. To clean up the bottom you will have to use the chisel with its bevel side down. The rest of the work of thinning the sides of the turkey call can be done with a jackknife. The lid of the whetstone box is a shallower duplicate of the bottom.

A whetstone box of hollowed wood was discovered on the Arctic island of Novaya Zemlya in the 1870s along with a parcel of other ship's carpenter's tools. It had been left there by the survivors of a Dutch expedition that had been wrecked on the island in 1596 while in search of the Northeast Passage to China. This "whetstone" box (it was empty, so we must leave a little room for doubt

Five bits (left to right): Forstner, spoon, shell or nose, Jennings, center.

Clean out the waste with the chisel.

as to its use as such) shows no traces of prehollowing with an auger; the hollowing was done entirely with a chisel. Otherwise, it looks about like any other whetstone box, with the addition of a short extension to which a string is tied. Its owner probably kept it tied to his belt as he went about his duties, rather than leave it back on his workbench.

I have no idea how far back turkey calls go. Turkeys are birds of the New World and were of course unknown to the Europeans before they arrived. The Indians called them by blowing through a length of wingbone to produce similar sounds.

The cedar turkey call is of interest to me because it employs one of the less common ways of making sounds with wood. You hear this sound a lot when you're working on old buildings. Squeaking floorboards make their sound in the same way. When you work a big auger through a red cedar post, the persistent squeaking gets everyone's attention. Out in the forest you'll sometimes experience a jolt of adrenaline when the wind causes two tree limbs to rub against each other with the sound of an uncomfortably proximal banshee.

The resonant pitch of the turkey call when it is tapped on one side is reminiscent of African drums. In the nineteenth century, the Russian novelist Turgenev told in his *Hunting Sketches* about a traveling aristocrat who was forced to take shelter in a forester's cottage one stormy night. As they sat by the fire, the forester heard the faint sound of an axe ringing into a tree. A peasant was trying to steal firewood in the night under cover of the storm. By listening, the forester was able to discern the size and nature of the tree under the axe and went out after the peasant as his job required. (The story had a happy ending in that it was one of the earliest sympathetic views of the lower classes in the literature of the tsarist period.)

Even if you're not guarding (or poaching) the trees of the nobility, the tone of wood when it is struck can be useful to you. When you're hollowing a wooden bowl or dugout canoe, you can tell how thick the wood is by tapping it and listening to the tone. You can avoid buying or using a log or a beam that has a rotten spot concealed within it by listening with your ear against one end while someone strikes the other end with the poll end of an axe. The log should ring clearly, rather than give a dead muffled tone. It takes some experience, but you can usually tell a sound log by its timbre.

Unsound timber.

HURDLES

The New Englanders have a saying, when a man is in liquor,
he is making "Virginia Fences."

Thomas Auburey, *Travels Thru America* (1789)

"Bull strong, horse high, and pig tight," and the goats will still get through.

Fences, like houses, tell a lot about the people that made them. The stone walls and well-kept hedgerows of England speak of stability and long-established patterns. Early visitors to the booming American colonies derided the shabby appearance of the log houses and zigzag split-rail fences. The snake, or worm, fence was so characteristic of the new American landscape that it was commonly known as a "Virginia fence." This sort of fence gets its stability and its other names from the same source as the serpentine wall.

One great advantage of the snake fence is that it can be built with little more than an axe. You simply split a ten-foot length of log into rails and lay them crisscross on the ground—no post holes to dig or joints to cut. Since it has no permanent connection with the ground (it's best to raise each intersection up on a rock), the fence can be moved about at will or an opening made at any point. The simple snake fence becomes unstable after it reaches about ten rails high, but can still be raised higher by using crossed rails and riders at every intersection, or "lock." These add enough height to keep horses from jumping the fence.

One of my earliest encounters with principles of rural economy involved the snake fence. Passing a zigzag rail fence near Clifton Forge, Virginia, a friend, obviously echoing the words of his father, remarked, "Snake fences waste land." In one way I guess it's true: It's difficult to plow and plant in the zigs and zags. Grazing animals, though, get in there just fine, and the side away from the animals, which cannot be cut, becomes a refuge for wildflowers and birds. Even if the corners can't be cultivated, some stray seed is bound to take hold

Splitting rails.

there. The best corn and the best tobacco I remember was that which had to be handpicked because it grew in the "jamb of the fence."

As appropriate as the snake fence was to a new world, it was, like the log house, something new and unfamiliar to the English mind. If you think about it, a snake fence is simply a log house that has been stretched out. For an Englishman the more familiar manner of house building was to use upright posts with holes cut through them to receive the horizontal beams. This is the way he built houses, doors, and windows, and it is how he built fences.

A straight-line, post and rail fence is not self-supporting, and holes must be dug. This was originally done with shovels alone and later with the iron pikes and dipper spoons that preceded the now-familiar posthole digger.

The posts must be made from the heartwood of a resistant species if

they are to endure. Cedars, chestnut, walnut, sassafras, catalpa, and Osage orange are all commonly used for posts. One most-favored wood is the black locust, which is reputed by some to last two years longer than stone. Others say that it will last twice as long as the hole. One man even claimed that it will last two lifetimes—and says he knows cause he's seen it.

The ends of the posts are often charred in a fire in an attempt further to protect them from decay. The utility of this activity is questionable, however, as the only effect is to sterilize the wood if fungi is already present. The charcoal on the burned surface of the wood will not decay, but it has no strength and is not an effective barrier against the decay organisms always present in the soil. At most, charring buys an extra year or so.

Once the vertical posts are set in the ground, the rails must be set between them. Fixing the rails to the posts with nails would not make a very strong connection. This is a practicable method only when fencing with lighter sawn boards.

Rails need to be housed in holes or mortices through the posts, and there lies the problem with this type of fence. Chopping the narrow holes through the uprights is not an easy task, but this is largely the way it was done until the advent of the spiral auger at the end of the eighteenth century. Earlier augers were nowhere near as easy to use as the spiral auger with the center lead screw. The spiral auger will start easily on a curved surface and pull itself on through, enabling one to work faster and on rougher wood. Simply bore two holes and split out the wood in between to make the mortice. Then thin down the ends of the rails with an axe, and assemble.

Both the snake fence and the post

Cultural mixing in the New World, log houses and post-and-rail fences.

Boring the holes for a new post.

and rail fence have their analogues in portable fences called hurdles. Used mainly for folding sheep and other small stock, they are more common in Britain than on this side of the Atlantic. One reason for this is the difference in agricultural practices between here and there. The crowded isles need much greater control and more intensive land-use practices than have been necessary in the comparative vastness of America. Still, hurdles are useful anytime it is necessary to move animals about and still maintain control over them, as when we take the goats into town for market day on the green. We are often

set up near the vegetable stalls, and a strong pen is essential.

There are two sorts of hurdles, the woven wattle hurdle and the five-bar gate hurdle. The wattle hurdle is the elder of the two. As they are woven rather than jointed their manufacture requires only the most minimal tools, little more than a sharp blade. The production of wattle hurdles is associated with a specific sort of woodland growth called "coppice." Coppice refers to the forests of shoots that arise from the still-living stumps of harvested timber. Even when trees were too large to be used effectively with primitive tools, one could always kill

the upper part of the tree by ringing the trunk with an axe. The well-developed root system of the tree would then put all of its energy into sending up sprouts from the stump and roots. These shot up quickly and hence were very straight, knot free, and easily worked by hand splitting.

Like willow for basketry, coppice wood for hurdles was first harvested from the wild and then later cultivated to ensure a steady source of high-quality material. In Tudor England the wool industry (and, hence, sheep control) became so important that hazelwood coppices were established solely for the production of wattle

Chop out the waste with a mortice axe.

Framed timbers with woven wattle and daub infilling are typically English forms.

hurdles. Careful management can keep a coppice productive for generations. The usual rotation, or lapse between harvests, is seven years. Production hurdle makers must work close to the coppice, as the weaving requires the wood to be fresh, green, and pliant.

The tools of the wattle hurdle maker are a heavy hooked knife called a billhook and a 7-foot-long heavy timber with ten holes bored at equal intervals along its length to hold the uprights in place while the weaving goes on. This timber, or at least the pattern of holes for the uprights, is best made in a curve to keep the

hurdle stiff as it is being woven. Curved, it can support a considerable weight; left flat it would buckle immediately. When the completed hurdle is removed from the timber and stacked to dry, the curve flattens out and the tension holds the weaving tight.

There is another trick to making hurdles, or any other item that involves making a sharp bend back on the stock. When you turn the split-hazel weavers about the end uprights, give them a solid spiral twist as you bend them back around. This twist makes the fibers of the wood behave as though they were a rope and al-

lows them to take the bend without splintering.

The bottom and top courses of the weaving need to be different from the infilling. Two rods are intertwined around the uprights, like a multistrand rope with sticks stuck through it. The uprights on either end need to be somewhat stouter than the other eight and left longer and pointed on their bottom ends so that they may be driven into the ground to hold the hurdle up.

I don't get much call for wattle hurdles and it's a good thing, for the material to make them is not generally available. Gate hurdles, however, are

The hurdle will be inverted for use when completed.   *Twist on the return.*

always in demand; the sheep people can never get enough. A hurdle of any kind needs to be both strong and light. Cleft oak provides the best combination of strength, light weight, and decay resistance. All the parts are split rather than sawn from the log, preserving the integrity of the grain from end to end, flowing around any knots or bends. To equal their strength in sawn material one would need pieces of greater dimension and weight, which would require more energy to make and move about.

Making gate hurdles is a pleasant undertaking from start to finish. They are generally 6 feet long by 3 feet

high. Start with fresh white-oak logs (other species will do, but this is all that I have ever used) in 6-foot lengths. Split the log in half, and then in half again, and so on. Once you get down to pieces about a handbreadth thick, you can start and open the split with the wedge, axe, or froe enough to get in a hand and a foot and tear it apart. Keep splitting until you have all the bars that you will need, five or six for each hurdle, measuring about 2½ inches by ½ inch. Failed lengths can be used for the braces and center uprights. The stout end posts should be made 1 inch by 2½ inches and 4 feet long. All the stock should be

heart of oak; any white sapwood left on will quickly lead to rot and ruin.

All the posts will be morticed in the same manner, so you will save time by making a guide stick with notches or nails at the appropriate points to speed the layout. Leave about 10 inches on the bottom of the posts—the part that will go into the ground—before the slot for the bottom rail and about 4 inches above the mortice for the top rail. Since young, unruly animals are usually short as well, the bottom rails need to be spaced closer together than those toward the top.

The mortices can be quickly chopped out with a chisel in the fresh

Five-bar hurdles.   *Bore the ends of the mortices in the uprights.*

wood, but another way, and one that I quite enjoy, employs a brace and bit and what is called a hurdle maker's twivil. It is called a twivil or twibil because it is a double-ended tool with two "bills." One of the ends of the T-shaped tool is shaped like a sharply hooked chisel; the other, like a broad knife. To make the mortice, bore two spaced holes through the post at the ends of where each mortice is to go. Then, with the hooked end of the twibil, reach in one of the holes and lever out the wood in between. It may take two or three bites to get it all out. Clean up any mess that is left with the knife end.

When the mortices are chopped with a chisel, the post needs to be firmly supported on a bench or stump. When working with a bit stock and twibil, however, you can hold the work by springing it between two horizontal bars and the top of a small stump. This holds the post firmly and gives the hook of the twibil and the knife space to work through without hitting the bench top.

When all the posts have been morticed through, chop their bottom ends to points to go into the ground and knock the corners off the top end to center the blows from the mallet used to drive them into the ground. Now

set the rails in place with a half inch or so of their ends protruding through the mortices. The top rail, the bottom rail, and the third rail from the bottom are held in their mortices by oak pegs driven through holes bored through the sides of the posts. The other rails can be left free.

The center upright and the diagonals are held to the rails by nails that are clinched over on the back side. The best sort of nail for this is what is called a "clout" nail. They are designed to punch through the wood without splitting and, upon hitting an iron plate placed on the underside of the two pieces to be joined, to clinch

Clean out with the twivil.

themselves. Clout nails should be available through hardware dealers, but wire nails will do just as well if you must use them. They may tend to split the wood, but this can usually be avoided by blunting the point or pre-drilling the hole. Get the center upright in first and then place the diagonal braces by eye.

Hurdles will support themselves; the pointed bottom ends of the uprights can be forced into the ground by the weight of your foot on the lower rail. The tops of the uprights may be joined by cords or wire loops.

A more permanent structure can be had by driving stouter posts into the ground at the juncture of each pair of hurdles.

When I lived in New Mexico, I once made about a half mile of the woven type of fencing—at the strong suggestion of my non-goat lover neighbors, who stressed the importance of hemp gardening to the local economy. I spent several weeks cleaving, weaving, and pounding wood, winding my way between the aspen trees. When the task was finally done, the relieved community of gardeners gathered to watch the herd's reaction to its new home. Someone produced a cardboard sign to tack over the gate which read, "Abandon hope all ye who get out of here." Florence, the defiant queen nanny of the herd, promptly danced up on her hind legs, seized the sign, and ate it down. I should have known.

One week and three devastated gardens later, the wide-eyed goats and my exhausted self decided that it might be healthier back East. The ten thousand fences between us and my outraged neighbors just might be enough.

WHIMSY DIDDLING

I can feele A whimsey i' my bloud.

Ben Jonson, *Volpone* (1605)

Toys in the family. The mechanical ones are by my sister Barbara and the ball in the cage by Great-uncle Graham.

Old wooden cigar boxes were still generally available when I was a kid. I remember asking for them at the counter at my father's pool hall down by the Washington Navy Yard. The thin, soft, aromatic wood from these boxes was great for making all kinds of things. My favorite were little stern-wheeler paddleboats. With my coping saw, I cut the bow to a V and the stern to a U-shaped fork to hold the paddle wheel, with its two interlocked blades. Propelled by a rubber-band motor, it would putter across a puddle. Making them, though, was the greater pleasure.

These boats are part of a whole class of toys of sticks and strings that are largely got out with the coping saw. I never spent much time developing skills in the toy department, but my sister did. Barbara makes mechanical toys, cutting the outline with a coping saw and then carving in the details with a knife (the same way a Chippendale chair is made). Working primarily with wood gleaned from old crates and other odd pieces that people find and save for her, she has made virtually every wooden toy known, but my two favorites are the acrobat and the log cutters. Working from the traditional patterns, she personalizes them with a likeness of the recipient's face.

The acrobat is a simple jointed figure suspended between two uprights that flips about when the twist in a cord through its arms is undone by stretching. I'm sure the idea for this must have come from the winding cord on bow saws—or perhaps it was the other way around. The rubber-band motor of the paddleboat is simply a modern version of this.

Another variation on this theme is the "buzz saw." This is simply a disc with two holes drilled through the center and a looped cord passed through the holes. To make ready, the cord is twisted with the disc in the

middle. When the ends of the cord are pulled apart, the disc spins and the cord unwinds and then rewinds, lengthening and shortening like an elastic band. Holes drilled along the periphery of the disc will cause it to emit a peculiar whirring sound as it is spun.

This same motion has been used in making an interesting return spring for cord-driven lathes. The disc in this case is elongated into a spool that is suspended by the doubled line strung on an archer's bow. The drive cord is wound on the spool so that when it is pulled, the spool rotates, the string on the bow is twisted and shortened, and the bow is bent. The return is smooth, and the mechanism is compact.

Whimmy Diddles

An awful lot can be done with a jackknife. One dry, windy spring while

I was still in school, there were terrible forest fires up in the mountains. About mid-morning one day my classmates and I were called to go in as a relief crew for the regular fire fighters. For the entire week that we were in the mountains, however, we were kept in reserve, being thrown into the breach only for after-midnight mop-ups and village-idiot scrub fires. The days were spent sitting on the grass outside the ranger station in the valley. By the second day, boredom had reduced us to a state of abject stupefaction. Most of us had pocket-knives, and the hills about us were covered with mountain laurel. So it wasn't long before someone started whittling, and somehow we got started on what must have been the largest gee-haw whimmy diddle whittling binge in history. A gee-haw whimmy diddle is a stick with notches cut along its length and a propeller on one end. When you rub the corrugated length just right with another stick, the propeller begins to spin. The gee-haw part of the name refers to the directions shouted to oxen to steer them to the right or left. By skillful guidance, you can get the propeller going to the right or left as you wish. Few toys are more strongly associated with the mountain folk tradition than the gee-haw whimmy diddle.

These things are awfully simple to make. You just need a knife and a pencil-sized length of hard twig. Trim a half inch of the end down to smaller than a match stick, leaving the very end fatter in a little bulge to keep the propeller from flying off. The propeller is a piece about an inch long trimmed down in the middle thin enough that you can work a hole through it with the point of your knife. The hole must be just big enough to force over the swelling on the end of the stick, leaving the propeller to spin freely on the shaft. The notches are

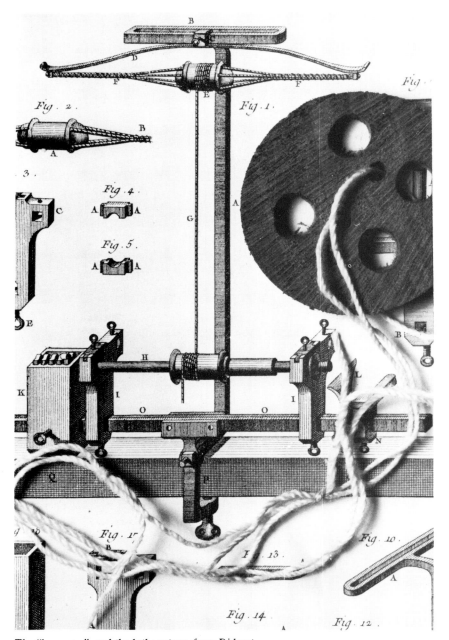

The "buzz saw" and the lathe return from Diderot.

Willow Whistles

After two days of heavy whimmy diddling, even their elusive charm was wearing thin. Several people had gone nuts, taking multiforked twigs and making Medusa-headed devices with as many as five or six propellers going at once. I, for one, was getting desperate. We were supposed to stay close to the ranger station in case we were needed in a hurry, and as luck would have it, there was a stream across from the station with a weeping willow on the opposite bank. As soon as I saw it, I knew we would be able to make it for another day or so. I waded into the ice-cold water far enough to break off a half dozen of the long green whips and headed back to the station.

Willow whistles can only be made in spring and early summer, when the tree is growing strong. This job requires bright green twigs with long spaces between the bumps, or nodes, where the leaves come out. The fresher and greener and fatter and smoother the piece, the easier the whistle will be to make. A sharp knife is the only tool needed. Find a long space between the nodes and cut it out by rolling it between a flat surface and the knife blade.

A whistle whistles when a jet of air is directed at the edge of an opening in the chamber. Differential air pressure causes the air stream to oscillate on either side of the edge, somewhat in the manner of a fluttering flag. Make this edge in the willow whistle by first making a perpendicular cut through about one-third the diameter of the willow about ¾ inch in from one end. Then cut down from the far end at about a 35-degree angle and remove the little chip.

To make the chamber, you need to take out the insides of the twig, and for this the green willow is very obliging. In the spring the layer of cells

evenly spaced down the midsection to the fore end of the stick. The scratching stick appears to work best when it is sliced to a V-shaped cross section, although some prefer to leave theirs round.

There is a lot of argument and conjecture about effective design in weighting the ends of the propeller and spacing the notches and the proper way to hold the thing. This is what makes it such a good toy: it takes skill and involvement to operate, the sound and action are gratifying, and you can't for the life of you figure out how the darn thing works.

On with the propeller.

Gee.

between the bark and the wood is rapidly growing and dividing, and it is very fragile. You can crush this cambium layer by gently rolling the willow between a flat surface and the side of your jackknife. Don't press too hard or you can crush or tear the bark as well. When you feel that you have rolled over every spot, place the end grain of the stick on the corner of something and push down firmly on the bark as if to slide it off. The crushed layer of cells should give with a snap, and the bark can be slid off the stick. If it doesn't give, you can try rolling a bit more. If it still doesn't

work, it's the wrong time of year. The expression "clean as a whistle" is said to come from the pure whiteness of this inner stick.

Set the bark aside and cut the stick in twain by rolling the knife blade on it right where the first perpendicular cut was made. The shorter of the two pieces will become the ramp, or fipple block, which funnels and directs the air at the angled cut in the bark. Slice this short piece lengthwise, taking off one-quarter of its diameter on one end and angling to about one-half the diameter on the other. Push this piece back into the bark, larger end first, so

that it will aim the air right at the sharp angle. Stick the other piece of the stick a short ways into the back end of the bark and you're in business. You can change the pitch of the whistle by sliding the long stick in and out.

Once you get the hang of it, you can turn out a whistle in about a minute. This was our fourth day with nothing to do, and it wasn't long before every one of us was armed with a brace of willow whistles and attempting to play them all at once. They are shrill devils, and I guarantee that if you get twenty people all tuning

Cut between the nodes.

A sharp knife is essential.

Clean as a whistle.

Cut where the first vertical slice was made.

and playing willow whistles while simultaneously rattling away on their multiheaded whimmy diddles, you can crack even the most hardened mountain forest rangers. Within an hour they had scrounged together a set of horseshoes and a volleyball, putting an end to our whittling diversions. The willow whistles had dried out by late that afternoon and were unplayable. We later traded all the whimmy diddles to one of the rangers for ramps (wild mountain onions) and venison. A few of us were even called on that evening to help put out a fire—and we just about beat that barbeque grill into the ground.

Cut the fipple and put it back in.

Turning the prebored whistle with the aid of plug centers.

Turned Toys

The number of different toys based on the simple principle of axial symmetry is unbounded. To some, such as toy soldiers, the turnery lends a delightful abstraction; to others, like croquet balls and spinning tops, the symmetry is its essence.

One of the simplest and earliest toys of childhood is a rattle made up of captive rings on a single piece of wood. This toy is greatly beloved by novice turners, as it looks much harder to do than it is. You simply chuck up a semidry piece of beech, birch, or what have you, in the lathe, cut rings, and then undercut until they are free. Slide the free ring to

one side and clean out underneath. This sort of captive ring turnery is a standard production item for Mexican artisans, who make the most elaborate chocolate stirrers on a bow lathe in minutes.

Just to give you more ideas for toys from the lathe, a croquet set is all turnery, as are tops, yo-yos, baseball bats, ten pins, and the elusive Bilboquet, the cup and ball game that can give you such a fit.

One final item for the lathe. If it's the wrong time of year for willow whistles, you can make terrible loud turned whistles. This is a good use for scraps of attractive wood that are too small for anything else.

The concept of how the whistle works is of course the same for both willow and wooden whistles. These,

however, are a lot more durable. It's best to bore out the length of the whistle first and then turn true to this axis. Just about any sort of bit will bore through end grain, although if it is not correctly sharpened it cannot be forced simply by pushing harder, as it can through side grain. I have found ⅜ inch to be a good size for the hole.

If you are using a spring-pole lathe, you can easily set the conical centers in the openings at either end of the rough blank and turn away. On a wheel-driven lathe, you will probably need to fashion a set of plug centers. These act as false ends to center the prebored hole precisely on the lathe. To make them, set a conveniently sized piece of good hardwood in your lathe and turn it down in the middle to

The finished whistle in the company of toys from town turners.

the same diameter as the hole. Then remove it from the lathe, saw it through in the middle, and insert the pieces into the two ends of the whistle blank. After securing the whole affair in the lathe, you are ready to turn the whistle to the pattern that you want. This is the same procedure that I use when turning wheel hubs to ensure that the circumference and shaft hole are concentric.

Cut the angled air outlet with a fine saw. You will make a much cleaner cut if you push a filler rod into the saw cut before you start sawing. Clean up the cut with a chisel before you pull the rod out, and it will be perfect. If the rod is a tight fit, you can use it to make the fipple block to direct the air flow right at the sharp edge. The end where you will blow should be a half section of the rod, sloping to a three-quarter section at the other end. The far end of the whistle must be stopped to close the air chamber. You can use either a fixed block or a sliding one, which will allow you to vary the pitch.

We tend to pass off things like whimmy diddles with little thought, just as the pre-Columbian Mexican Indians gave little thought to the terra-cotta toys with wheels on them that they made for their children. They had the wheel for toys, but there is no evidence that they used it in other activities, not for even so much as a wheelbarrow. Perhaps some future civilization will ponder how strange it was that people used the whimmy diddle only as a toy and never harnessed the awesome power hidden within it.

C H A P T E R 9

TWO TOOLS

I schall merke well upone the wode
And kepe his mesures trew and gode
And so, by my mesures all,
To the full wele my mayster schall.

"The Debate of the Carpenter's Tools" (fifteenth century)

I would not venture to guess when the first string was rubbed with charcoal and snapped to make a straight line, but I wouldn't want to try and build a respectable ziggurat without a snap line. Remember, too, that in the eighth century B.C., Homer had Odysseus hewing "true to the line."

Almost as simple is the marking gauge, which will scribe a line precisely parallel to a given surface. These are two tools that you need to have, and making them is good practice for working with both fresh-cut and seasoned wood. The snap-line reel can be whittled from a stick of green stove wood with a jackknife as you wait for the bath water to get hot. The marking gauge, though, can be as much an exercise in precision cutting and joining as you want it to be.

A line reel from Japan.

The Snap Line

It is hard to conceive of a tool that could replace the snap line. In the Oriental tradition, ink rather than a dry pigment is used. Their snap-line reels, with their integral ink pots, are often beautifully carved. The most common reels in the West, though, are those that spin on a shaft that is extended to form the handle. The pigment is rubbed on from a solid or held in a separate container. Sometimes the equipment can be quite minimal, as little as a hollow chopped in the end of a timber and filled with charcoal and water through which the string is run as it is unwound from a stick.

Line reels have taken many different forms, but one form was apparently very popular at one time, judging from the numbers that I have seen in collections. This is the U-shaped bow with its two stretchers pierced by the handle or axle. Old reels of this type are invariably stained a deep reddish brown from

the Venetian red or ochre that was used as a marking medium and worked in to the hickory by generations of sweaty hands. Charcoal and these earth-red colors are cheap and have been for a long time. In the late summer I always use pokeberry juice. It makes a brilliant purple line (beware, though, it's poisonous). I also save chunks of willow charcoal to rub directly on the string (charcoal burned from other woods is too hard to rub on). Blue chalk appears to be distinctly modern.

I have worked only with hickory when making these reels, but ash and similar woods would do as well. These tools get an awful lot of knocking about, and a brittle wood like cherry would not be a good choice. I have seen our hickory reels have logs rolled on them, but I have never seen one broken.

The Bow

You are better off using fresh green wood than trying to steam bend dried-out stock. When wood dries thoroughly, the lost flexibility can be only partially restored by steaming. Cleave a piece for the bow to just over ¾ inch wide by ½ inch thick by 14 inches long. With drawknife or jackknife, shave a 4-inch length of both ends to a uniform ¾ inch wide by ⅜ inch thick. The 6-inch midsection that will be bent around can now be shaved or whittled to just under ¼ inch thick, but leave it as wide as the two ends. To get an even bend, the change in thickness between the ends and the middle must be rounded, not abrupt. Using your knife as a scraper, pushing the blade along at just less than 90 degrees to the work, is a good way to get an even thickness.

To find the points to bore the holes to receive the tenons on the ends of the stretcher bars, measure in from each end 1 inch and 3½ inches. The greenness of the wood that makes it

Shave the bow with your jackknife.

A center bit is less likely to split the wood.

easy to shape and bend also makes the wood easy to split accidentally. A ⅜-inch auger pulling through a piece of hickory this size can easily cause it to crack. You can prevent this by clamping the sides as you bore the holes or by leaving the ends of the bows long and wide and shaving them down to the final dimensions only after the holes are bored. A "center bit" is less likely to split the wood than a regular spiral auger.

The two stretcher bars are best split out of one piece of wood. Cleave or whittle down a piece of wood to ¾ inch square by 3½ inches long. Bore a ⅜-inch hole through the middle of this piece and then split it in half. When the stretchers have been bored and separated, whittle a ½-inch-long, ⅜-inch-diameter tenon in the center of each end by alternately cutting square across the grain to form the shoulder and slicing down to this cut from the end.

Bending and Brashness

Test bend the bow and if it seems to need more flexibility, boil up some water and set the bow either over it or in it. I have helped wood along many a time by wetting it down and heating it over a fire made from a few handfuls of shavings on the ground.

I have also on occasion, when bending wood like this for sled runners and skis, encountered "brash" hickory that, in spite of everything I could do, snapped in two like fresh celery. Brash wood, when it breaks, snaps clean without long splinters. Brashness is often found in slow-grown wood with very narrow rings. Excessive heating can cause this sort of failure to occur in normal wood too,

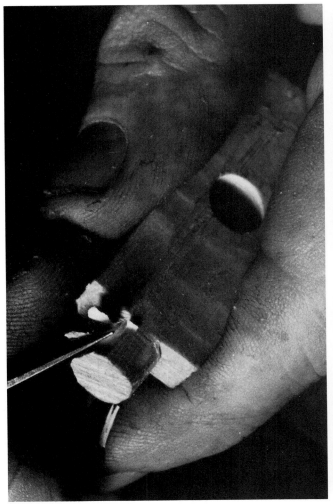

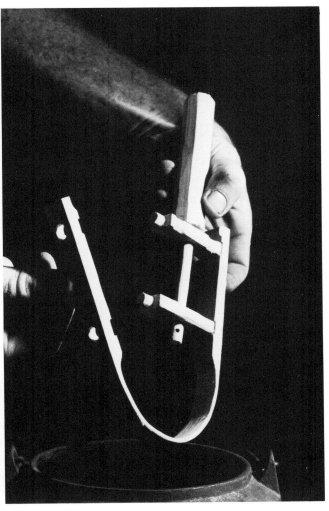

Make two stretcher bars.

Boiling water helps the bend. Note the seats cut in the bow to take the ends of the bars.

so go easy on the flames. Bring the bow around evenly, forcing any reluctant point with your thumbs. When the ends of the bow are seated on the stretchers, take a string and tie it to one of the sides and begin wrapping it around. Set this all aside and begin the handle.

The handle blank is cleft 7¼ inches long and ⅞ inch square. The part for your hand is 3¾ inches long and can be shaved to an octagon by taking off the corners evenly all the way around. The shaft is essentially a ⅜-inch-diameter, 3½-inch-long tenon. You whittle it in the same way that you did the tenons on the stretchers, pushing the knife in around the shoulder of the tenon and then slicing down to it. It's similar to chopping a tenon with a hatchet except that the knife blade is driven by pressure rather than by impact.

After slicing the excess off the shaft and shaving it smooth, stick the handle through the holes in the stretchers and mark it where it extends above the second stretcher. Then remove it and bore the match-stick-sized hole for the tiny seasoned peg that holds the handle on. Finally, take the reel in hand and chamfer the unnecessary corners away with your knife. Wind on cotton or linen line, tie on the toggle, and move on to the next job.

The Gauge

The marking gauge is apparently much more modern than the snap line. No evidence has been found to show that it was used by ancient Roman carpenters. The "skantyllyon" mentioned in the fifteenth-century poem "The Debate of the Carpenter's

A captive-wedge marking gauge and a thumb-screw cutting gauge.

cut a rabbet for, say, picture frames by gauging from both sides of a corner.

Most factory-made gauges adjust by means of a thumbscrew. But such gauges are dangerous, and I rarely use them in my shop. The problem is that thumbscrews have a magnetic attraction for people. Visitors can't seem to resist picking up a gauge and fiddling with the thumbscrew adjustment. It seldom occurs to them that I might have been relying on the setting that, unbeknownst to me, they have just changed. What havoc such fiddling has wrought.

The alternative method of securing the fence is the captive wedge—so called because the wedge has a stop to prevent it from falling free when loosened to change the setting. Most gauges with captive wedges have them set in parallel with the shaft. The wedge is set by hand pressure and further tightened by tapping the end of the shaft on a solid surface. Early gauges of the seventeenth century commonly had no wedge at all. They relied instead on snugness to hold the setting. A wedge was resorted to only when the fence would "slide not stiff enough" on the shaft. This expedient soon became standard, and a special slot was made for the wedge to slide in.

Most gauges are made from birch, beech, or box. Apple, pear, or plum will also do very well. Gauges born in cabinet shops may be of various exotics like rosewood or lignum vitae. Those from the carpenter's yard may be of pine or oak. Continental gauges are often made of hornbeam. As you can see, most any good wood will do.

The average gauge (if there is such a thing) has a shaft about 10 inches long and ¾ inch square. The fence is about an inch thick and between 2½ and 3½ inches square. More refined gauges (they can be objects of simple beauty) employ a shaft that is oval on one or more of its four faces. The

Tools" is likely an early form of the marking gauge though.

With a marking gauge and planes rough stock can be turned into precision plank in a trice. You simply plane one face true and then use the gauge to mark the opposing face exactly parallel to the first. Plane this face true and then repeat the process on the sides. A basic gauge with an added marking tooth enables one to

lay out mortice and tenon joints with ease and accuracy. Such a double-toothed gauge is in fact known as a morticing gauge. A gauge with a knife blade for the tooth is called a cutting gauge, which will cut deep into the wood instead of just scratching the surface. A cutting gauge can slice a clean shoulder across the grain of a raised panel, separate thin boards by cutting in from both sides, and even

Full-sized disassembly of the marking gauge in the previous photograph.

chisel out, even without precutting the sides with a saw. More often than not, the wedge is oriented so that as the fence is pushed away from the tooth, the grip is tightened rather than loosened. Make the wedge slot with a narrow chisel, and angle it to match the slope of the wedge. As for the wedge itself, avoid exposed sharp corners that could lead to fractures.

A French pattern, and one which I prefer for general carpentry, uses a wedge set in through the width of the fence at right angles to the shaft. The wedge is tightened or loosened by holding the gauge by the shaft and tapping the wedge itself on a hard surface. Adjustments are solid and quickly changed, which is important when you are doing jobs like planing a stack of rough-sawn floorboards to random widths determined by the narrowest point of each individual board.

This arrangement is quite simple to do. Instead of cutting a slot in line with the shaft hole, you bore a ⅜-inch-diameter hole through the width of the fence. This hole must be accurately placed at an angle partially to intersect the shaft hole. It is best first to bore this wedge hole through the sides of the fence and then bore the shaft hole through the face to just hit its edge. When you enlarge the shaft hole with the chisels, increase the amount of intersection to about ⅛ inch.

It would be troublesome to square up such a deep narrow hole. Fortunately, there is no need to do so. Simply make the wedge round to match the hole and cut a tapered flat on one side to give the wedge action. Make this dowel-wedge longer than necessary and then trim it off to protrude only ¾ inch on either end once you have tried it in place.

The tooth (or teeth if you are making a morticing gauge) is simply a small nail driven in at about ½ inch back from the end of the shaft. Cut

face with the tooth is best made oval because as the gauge is used, it is generally rocked forward to drag the tooth behind.

At any rate, the design is not as critical as the execution. The fit of the fence on the shaft needs to be precise along the whole of its length. I have seen many a homemade gauge that would not hold on a certain range of measurements because the shaft was

not accurately and consistently sized.

Make the shaft hole through the fence by first boring it with a ¾-inch auger and then squaring it up with a chisel. The orientation of the grain of the fence is important. The pressure of the wedge must be exerted along the grain of the wood of the fence not across it. This of course prevents the wedge from cracking the fence open and makes the wedge slot easy to

A morticing gauge. Alternative designs use two independent arms and teeth for mortices of differing widths.

"French" wedge gauges.

The dowel wedge.

The brass cutting-gauge wedge.

the nail off about ¹/₁₆ inch above the surface by first nicking it on either side with a triangular file and then snapping it off. Sharpen the tooth on two sides to a knife edge in line with the direction the gauge will be pushed.

If you are making a cutting gauge, the common way to set the blade is to bore a preliminary round hole, square it with a chisel or a coping saw, and use a single, taper-square wedge. Another way to wedge the blade into the shaft is to bore a ³/₁₆-inch-diameter hole and make a split-cylinder wedge by hacksawing a short piece of brass brazing rod of equal diameter in half down its length. With a little filing, the semicylindrical pieces can be shaped to enable you to sandwich the blade, made from a piece of heavy hacksaw blade, between them. If carefully made, the blade and wedge arrangement can be pushed into the untapered hole and will sit as solid as you please.

Having these two tools in your kit gives you the power to define the rectilinear world. Trees become framing timbers; cleft billets, a chest of drawers. As you hold them now, their wood is coarse and bland. But the miles of line that you saw to dust will be measured in the growing depth of their patina of ochre, charcoal, resin, and sweat.

CANDLE STANDS AND THE SLIDING DOVETAIL

It snowed and snowed, the whole world over,
snow swept the world from end to end.
A candle burned on the table,
A candle burned.

Boris Pasternak, *Dr. Zhivago* (1958)

One February a few years back, terrible ice storms savaged the county, taking down a lot of well-loved trees. One elderly neighbor in town lost a huge walnut tree that fell and crushed her garden shed. The loss must have upset her, as she and the tree had grown up together, but practical as ever, she had one of the neighborhood kids fetch me and offered me the wood in exchange for cleaning up the mess and making her a little something from it. There were some fine logs in the tree, but we both knew that no sawmill would touch it for fear of the costly damage the buried nails and sundry spikes that often inhabit yard trees could do to their saws. It was a good deal for us both.

I get most of my good timber in trades of this sort. One of the best trades for walnut, cherry, or good maple logs is an arrangement that begins, "Let me have that dead tree and I'll make you a candle stand out of it." These classic and useful tables can be made in just a few hours by hand and foot power, so both parties do well in the bargain.

The basic candle stand consists of six parts—three legs, a pedestal, and the top and its supporting block. The stand that I make is in the Queen Anne style, with cabriole legs (meaning they are shaped like the leg of a leaping goat) and a lathe-turned, classical vase-shaped pedestal or column (for instructions on making a candle stand without using a lathe, see page 110). The connection between the legs and the column is formed by sliding dovetail joints. These joints are a neat trick: the legs slide up into the column from the bottom in a clever puzzle arrangement that is not hard to do but is very satisfying. The top and its supporting block are also turned out on the lathe, and there's a bit of a trick to them too.

Riving

Somewhere inside that tree is your candle stand; you just need to get it out. The largest piece of the stand is of course the top and must come from the largest part of the tree. Using the utmost care, split the largest log in half directly through the pith. A froe is helpful to keep the split straight, as any misdirected cracks could ruin the top. Split the better half again to yield a somewhat thicker board than you will need. This extra thickness will allow you to plane out the cupping bend to the bark side of the top that will inevitably occur with seasoning.

Now thoughtfully rive out the blanks for the legs, column, and block, again leaving them larger than the final dimensions. Take care to exclude any pith or doty sapwood from any of your pieces. Bring them a bit closer to the appropriate size with hatchet and drawknife and set them aside for a few days. In very dry weather the thick column stock is

The first split goes right through the center.

prone to severe checking, so keep an eye on it and move it to a more humid environment if problems develop. The leg blanks seldom give such trouble.

Turning

When turning a large disc like the top of a candle stand on a lathe, the usual procedure is to affix the blank to a metal faceplate which can be directly mounted on the lathe in place of the drive center. This arrangement, somewhat like a horizontal version of a potter's wheel, gives you clear access to the workpiece. The headstock bearings on my treadle lathe are not set up to take this sort of load, however, so I do all such turning "between centers," first turning the column to its finished shape and then using it as a mandrel to hold the block and top in the lathe as they are turned. One would have to use the same procedure when doing such turning on a spring-pole lathe, where a rope wrapped around the workpiece provides the drive. It works quite well.

The Column

The column must be of sufficient diameter to contain the joints for the three legs, but beyond that the design is constrained only by your taste. The use of the lathe already assures a certain symmetry, your eye being the final judge of the boldness or weakness of curve and countercurve. The top cylinder perhaps looks best when it is equal in diameter to the bottom one. Another mechanical consideration is to leave a slight collar on the bottom cylinder to delineate the upper limit of the leg joints. The column must be oriented on the lathe with its base to the drive center and not the

The base of the column must be against the drive center of the lathe.

other way around, for reasons that you will see as you go on. The top of the column must be turned to end in the 1-inch-diameter tenon that will hold the block that in turn will hold the top. Do any spin finishing that you intend to do to the column now, while it is still turning true. It may want to wobble if you wait.

When the column is done to your liking, turn your hand to the block and the top. On the inch-thick piece riven out for it, lay out the block with a compass, about 5 inches in diameter. Bore the 1-inch-diameter hole through the center and saw out the circumference as accurately as possible. Set this block on the tenon turned on the column and reset the whole works in the lathe. Scrapers with well-turned edges may be your best choice for the flat-grain turning required here. Turn the block ever so slightly concave on what will be its upper side. Diminish its thickness to the edges on its underside.

The Top

The top is not easily done on a foot-powered lathe except with care and preparation. Lay out the circle of the top with a compass, cut it out as closely as possible with your saw, and true up any obvious lopsidedness on the two faces with a plane or a draw-knife. Now take the block and drill three holes for the brass screws that will hold it to the top. The screw-heads must be countersunk into the block, and brass is best if you don't want to damage your turning gouges. If you don't want to use screws at all, you can join the two pieces with pegs secured by wedges, glue, or both. Center the previously turned block as precisely as possible on the point made by the compass center on the underside of the top and fasten it down. Push the assembly onto the tenon on the end of the column. You may need to saw off part of the tenon to get the block to sit tight.

Set the whole arrangement back in the lathe and work the face of the top about to find its center by trial and error. When it looks right, bring the lathe slowly up to speed. If there are problems with vibration, turn the piece slowly while holding a scribe against it to mark any out-of-round or off-center places. These should be removed by saw or shave, for any vibration will absorb a large portion of the energy you need for the turning. Remember that although the entire assembly—column, block, and top—is rotating at the same number of revolutions per minute, the surface speed is much greater at the larger diameters. A light touch is in order. Turn the top with an upturned lip around the edge. Do your finishing while it's still on the lathe and then take it all out and trim off the center bump.

Legs

Now for the legs. First bring the blanks to the appropriate thickness by planing one face level and then using a gauge to mark the parallel thickness and planing on the other side. Mine measure 1⅛ inches thick. Trace around a leg pattern copied from the photograph or a candle stand which you like on to one side of the blank. You need to arrange the pattern on the wood so that the narrowest part of the leg has the greatest run of straight, unbroken grain. Usually you can squeeze the legs quite close together in an intermeshing pattern to conserve material.

Separate the waste from the outlines of the legs with a turning saw, something like an oversized coping

Turn the block using the column as the mandrel.

Without a Lathe

You don't have to have a lathe to make this sort of stand. The pedestal can be shaped with planes or shaves to a polygon and the top cut out with saws. You usually do better by being honestly angular and not trying to imitate lathe work with shaving. For a three-legged stand you can shape the pedestal to a hexagon, easily done with the aid of dividers. On the end grain of the base of the pedestal blank, describe about a 3-inch-diameter circle. Now without changing the setting on the dividers, pace off around the circumference of the circle in six perfect steps. Plane flat away to lines connecting these points in a graceful arcing taper up to the square tenon cut to hold the top and block. The legs are joined to alternate facets of the hexagon with sliding dovetails just as on the turned version.

Lay out a hexagonal column with a pair of dividers.

saw. Lacking a turning saw, you can use a coping saw with the coarsest-toothed blade you can get.

Set one of the sawn-out blanks in the vise and begin shaping and smoothing the upper surface with the spokeshave. You will have to change directions of attack at the knee and instep of the leg to match the change of the grain. Usually this causes you to neglect the actual point of change, making a knobby knee, but you will notice and remedy this if it gets ugly.

The sweep of the curves on the upper side of the leg is usually gentle enough to allow you to reach the bottom of any concavity with a normal spokeshave. The underside, which will need trimming too, however, has a very tight inside curve which is best dealt with by cross-grained slicing with a gouge, preferably an in-cannel one with the bevel on the inside of its radius. The underside of the leg need not be rounded over like the top, but can be left somewhat unfinished. You may wish to do just the edges of the underside; the profile of the leg will appear finished to all but someone lying flat on the floor.

Sliding Dovetails

The legs attach to the column by means of dovetails that slide. These are no different from more familiar dovetails except that they are long and solitary. I cut the tails on the legs first and then custom cut their matching receptacles in the column.

If you have been careful in dimensioning the stock for the legs, you can lay out the tails very quickly by using cutting and marking gauges set to scribe the two dimensions of the dovetails. Use a cutting gauge for the long lines down the sides of the leg and you will have the first step of the most accurate means of sawing the shoulder of the dovetail already be-

Get the top as true as possible before going to the lathe.

Attach the block to the top.

Turn the top just as you did the block.

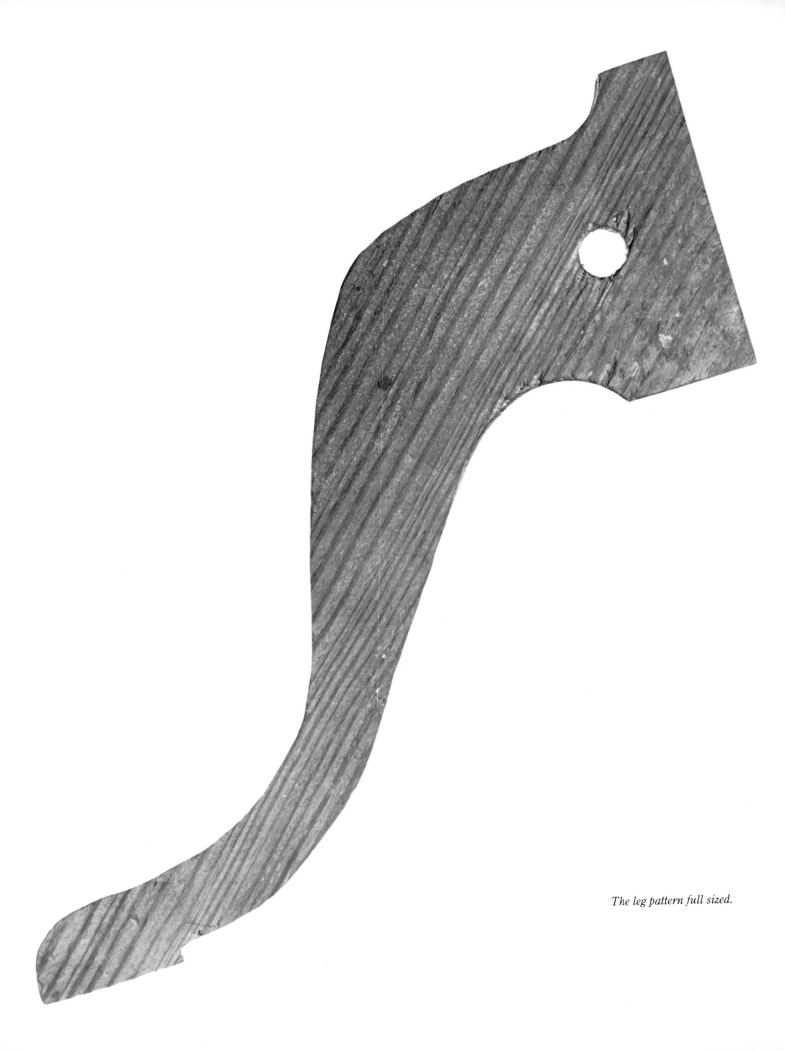

The leg pattern full sized.

Cut out the legs with a turning saw.

gun. Enlarge this incision to a tilted V by drawing a chisel down the waste side of this line and you have a slot in which to begin the saw cut without tearing any of the grain. Make these saw cuts on both sides of the leg down to the other set of gauge marks scribed on the end grain of the tails. Hold your bench chisel down flat and roll out shavings until you touch both the back edge of the leg and the bottom of the saw cut to make perfect tails.

All that remains now is to mate the dovetails on the legs to matching slots cut in the column. Clamp the column at a convenient angle in the vise and sweep the floor beneath it. With a clean floor you stand a better chance of retrieving any chip that may inadvertently break off. If you can find it, you can always glue it back on.

Hold the first leg on the side of the base of the column precisely where it will go and scribe down either side of the dovetail. At the upper limit of where the slot will stop in the column make a cross-grained saw cut that goes just deep enough to touch these two side lines. Slide a chisel up from the bottom to cut a flat on the column equal in length and width to the back of the dovetail on the leg. Set the top of the dovetail on the bottom end grain of the column, carefully aligned with the flat, and scribe around its outline. Remove the leg and with a straight edge continue the lines of the narrowest width of the dovetail up the length of the flat on the column.

Now, find the auger bit that most closely fits between the two lines and, at the upper limit of where the slot will go, bore down to the depth that the dovetail will reach. This hole will provide the stopping and clearance for the work to follow. Starting at the bottom, saw down the angle of the sides of the slot as best you can. A short backsaw will do best. Now, with a narrow chisel, slide along and

Lay out the dovetails on the finished legs with a cutting gauge.

Saw down to the gauge marks on the end and slice the dovetails with a chisel.

Scribe along the width of the dovetail down the base of the column.

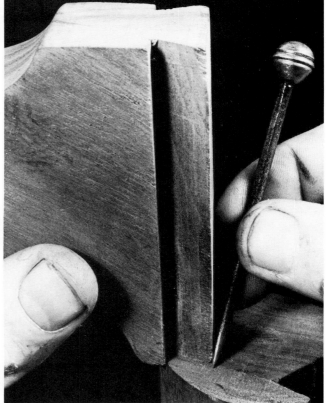

Scribe around the dovetail on the bottom.

Run the lines of the narrowest part of the dovetail down the flat and bore a hole at their end.

Saw down to the auger hole as best you can and split out the waste with a chisel.

Clean up with a bevel-edged paring chisel.

Finish the ends with a skew chisel.

Finishing

There is no substitute for careful work with sharp gouges and chisels in getting a proper finished surface on your lathe-turned work. If you maintain the bevel of the tool rubbing against the wood as you cut, the wood will already be burnished to a natural gloss. There are always places of course where you feel you must resort to fine abrasive paper or steel wool carefully applied while the wood is in motion, but such abrasive treatment may be avoided if you wish by burnishing with a handful of shavings held against the wood as it spins.

I do very little in the way of fine finishes and am prone just to slather on linseed oil and beeswax and rub until I can't stand it anymore. I think my shop is too dusty for shellac or varnish, but they are both traditional finishes as well. Oil or beeswax may be applied and polished while the work is spinning in the lathe. I get my wax from my own bees, so I am particularly fond of it as a finish. You can rub the solid block of wax against the spinning wood to apply it and then press a cloth against it so that the friction will melt it and force it into the wood. This is a rather soft finish and tends to waterspot easily. A more durable and easily accessible polish is carnauba wax applied in paste form and buffed to a gloss in the same manner.

Careful gouge and chisel work with the bevel rubbing leaves a burnished surface.

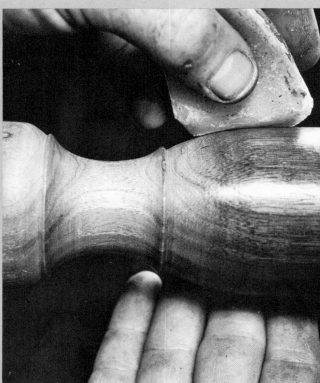

Melting in beeswax.

split out as much of the waste wood as you can. A bevel-sided paring chisel will help you clean up the sides and the bottom. The undercut top end of the slot is an odd reach that calls for an odd chisel called a skewed former. A well-made skew is a useful tool to have, but if one is not immediately at hand, you can grind a substitute from a bit of saw blade or an old chisel or do the job with the point of your jackknife. Keep checking and trying the fit until the leg slides up and stops with a click.

The first leg can be set in at any point on the circumference. Once it is in, you can eyeball thirds and continue the process until all the legs are in. Any error that will be noticed in the finished piece is likely to be in the vertical alignment of the legs rather than in gauging equal thirds. There is no reason not to glue the legs into place unless you just don't want to. If the fit is snug enough that they won't come loose of their own accord, you can leave them unglued and slide your dovetails in and out at will.

If you have never made fine furniture before, these candle stands are an excellent place to start. They look good, they're easy and useful, and you can make them from a tree with a story behind it. "Remember that old tree that used to stand over by . . ."

PLANES

I schalle clens on every syde
To helpe my mayster in his pride.

"The Debate of the Carpenter's Tools" (fifteenth century)

It is sometimes said that the use of the plane makes the distinction between the trades of carpentry and joinery. While a carpenter builds with timbers that are sawn or hewn, the joiner uses planed stock to make doors, windows, and staircases. The plane is used not only to smooth and dimension the material but often to form the actual means of joining. In America the division between the two trades has become less clear than it was in Britain, but the distinction is a good one to remember.

A plane works like a chisel sliding along the wood, taking off a shaving as it goes. The advantage of the plane is that it can be adjusted to take off a shaving of a constant thickness. But constancy is not all a plane has going for it. The wooden sole of the plane in front of the blade holds the wood flat until it is severed by the blade, preventing the wood from splintering or tearing out ahead of the cut. The flat sole also aids the plane in the performance of its essential function: the leveling of surfaces. The long body allows the iron to ride over low spots and remove only the high spots until the entire surface is flat.

The possibilities of shaping the sole and the iron of the plane to perform specific functions are endless. There are thousands of different patterns, from those that level and smooth a surface (rendering that surface a plane) to those that shape specific joints, the decorative moulding planes, and special planes for rounding, hollowing, and even connecting wooden water pipes. Since all planes function in a similar manner, the best foundation for successful work with any of them is to understand the workings of the simplest.

The most common and useful plane is the jack. About 16 inches long with an iron (the blade is called the iron even if it is steel) about 2 inches wide, it can be set up to work fine or coarse as the job requires.

Many early planes are of yellow birch, and Continental European ones may be of hornbeam, but beech is the most common choice because of its dimensional stability and smooth wearing. The oldest jack plane I have is an odd one, not in its shape but in its material—white oak. It is a well-made and straightforward tool with a single iron from the eighteenth-century maker James Cam. The body of this plane was most likely made by the man who intended to use it. The iron was probably purchased locally, but it originated in the factories in Sheffield, England. Local smiths could make plane irons, but those from England were usually better and cheaper.

Sharpening

To remove the iron from a wooden plane for sharpening, strike the fore end of the top of the body sharply with a wooden mallet as you support the plane with your free hand. Often a plane will have an inset "start" or "strike button" at this point whose purpose is to save the body of the plane from wear. On small planes the strike button may be on the rear, and that is where you should tap. A sharp rap will free the wedge and the iron so that it can be withdrawn.

Plane irons are chisel-edged tools in that they are beveled on only one side. They need to be not only razor

Rap the fore end to loosen the iron.

Curves of irons. Jointer at top, jack at bottom, and fore in the middle.

work with their bevels down toward the wood, it is essential that this bevel be flat rather than convex. To see the problem with a convex bevel, put your index finger on the page and push it forward as though it were a plane iron. Unless your fingernails are much longer than mine, the edge will not contact the page. This is exactly what happens with an ill-ground or dull plane iron.

When all the nicks are gone and you feel a wire-edge burr develop on the flat-side edge of the iron, the grinding is done. Take the iron and hone it on a fine whetstone, maintaining the bevel that you made in grinding. Be careful again not to create a convex bevel in honing. Some workers like to save time by grinding the iron to a 25-degree angle and then honing only the edge to 30 degrees. I see nothing wrong with this compound bevel and would perhaps use this method myself were it not for force of habit.

The flat side of the iron must remain flat right up to the very edge. Any rounding over on this side makes the edge quite blunt. To finish the honing, lay the flat side flat on the whetstone and give it a few strokes back and forth. Strop the edge on your palm or other leather and you're done.

The Cap Iron

Cap irons, or chip breakers, came along at the end of the eighteenth century. This new double iron for planes allowed one to plane difficult wood much more smoothly than was possible with the single iron. The chip breaker does exactly what its name implies. When a shaving is severed by the cutting iron, it slides up the face of the iron and can exert enough leverage to cause the wood to break out ahead of the iron. The chip

sharp but also properly shaped. The proper shape of the iron depends on how many planes you have and what you use them for. Ideally, one should have a set of four bench planes for working flat surfaces. A 16-inch-long jack plane would be the first on the job with its slightly convex iron. A fore plane from 18 to 24 inches long follows the jack; with its less convex iron it further levels the work. Finally, the jointer, from 2 to 3 feet long with an iron ground straight across and rounded only on the corners, will leave the surface dead smooth and level. The fourth plane, the little 8-inch-long smooth plane, does the same finishing action and has the same

straight iron shape as the jointer, but is used for jobs when the length of the jointer would be cumbersome. The cutting edge of these irons, no matter how shaped, needs to be aligned square to the sides of the iron. They may be convex or straight, but they must not be tilted to one side unless they are for a plane that is designed to use a skewed iron.

The shape and the bevel of the plane iron are created on the grindstone. The proper bevel for a plane iron is between 25 and 30 degrees. The 30-degree angle is reached when the length of the bevel is twice the thickness of the iron at the end of the bevel. Since common plane irons breaker prevents this by sharply flexing the shaving and breaking it before it can get long enough to do any harm.

The breaker iron is usually attached to the cutting iron by a screw which allows it to be removed for sharpening the cutter and reset at the proper distance from the edge. A jack plane may have the breaker as far back as 1/8 inch; a smooth or jointer should have a setback of only 1/32 inch. The smoother and finer the cut, the closer the breaker iron should be to the edge.

When you reset the breaker on the cutter, inspect it carefully to see that no gap remains between the two where shavings could lodge. If there is, they will, and the plane will choke.

Setting

The set of the iron determines the depth at which the iron will work—rank set (the iron protruding more from the sole) for coarse work, fine set for fine work.

Place the iron back in the throat of the plane, bevel down (unless it is a special low-angle plane, rare in wood), and push the wedge into its seat. Turn the plane upside down and sight along the sole to judge the squareness and depth of the iron. Set it a tiny fraction of an inch shallower than what you want and lightly tap the wedge home. The iron will usually travel a bit deeper with the wedge, so you need to anticipate this movement. If the iron appears to be too deep, a sharp tap on the heel end of the body will raise it. This loosens the wedge as well, so it will be wanting another tap. If the iron is too shallow, tap either on the front end grain of the body or on the top end of the iron itself. The wedge may again be loosened by tapping on the iron, so see that it is well secured before you try the plane out. Wooden-bodied planes,

The chip breaker in action.

like many simple tools, depend a lot on the finesse of the user.

Planing

Once the plane is tuned up, the iron sharp, and the sole flat, you're ready for the performance. Secure the stock on the bench and be sure that it is well supported along its whole length. If the wood flexes under the pressure of the planing, the plane will not cut true. This is particularly important in long or thin stock. A good height for a planing bench is between 29 and 31 inches off the floor.

The wood that you're working on

has everything else to do with how well the plane will work. Clear, dry, straight-grained stock will plane sweetly and flow in long rolls from the throat. The iron can be set rank to work such stock down rapidly. Knotty, contrary, curly grained, or damp wood requires a finely set iron. The progression for bringing a piece true begins with a rank-set plane and ends with one set to take shavings thinner than paper.

Before you begin, sight down the board and look for any obvious high spots. You will attack these directly. Hold the plane with your right hand on the "tote," or handle, your left hand around the fore end of the stock, thumb on the near side. Start planing.

Tap the nose for a deeper cut.

Do not slide the plane back across the surface on the return stroke; this quickly dulls the iron. Rather, lift the rear slightly so that the iron is clear of the work on the return.

Work your way to the end, taking off the obvious high spots as you go. Sight down the board again and see how you've done. Once you have brought down the mountains with a jack plane, set it down on its side (to protect the iron and as a measure of respect for the tool) and begin on the surface with a jointer. The long jointer, which spans 30 inches or more, uses its length to bring the surface down to a true plane. The long sole of the jointer will span any low spots, holding the iron above them until the last of the risings is done in and the surface is level.

Technique in jointing is everything.

Start the plane with the iron off of the wood, the fore end of the sole resting on the wood. Put all your pressure on your left, forward hand as you start. As the whole of the sole comes into contact with the surface, put equal pressure on both hands for the pass along the board. When you reach the far end of the board, shift the greater pressure to the rear hand as the fore end of the sole heads off. It's like swinging a baseball bat. You must start in the proper position, swing and put your body into it, and follow through. The bat is swung in an arc; the plane, in a straight line.

You can hear the progress of the plane as you work. On each pass down the board the silences as the iron rides over hollows grow shorter. The lengths of the unbroken shavings become longer and longer until the

Jointing.

Baileys

In the mid-nineteenth century, one Leonard Bailey of Boston, Massachusetts, developed and patented a metal, cam-action locking lever to secure plane irons. A few years later he came up with a cast-iron body to mount on the wooden stock which allowed the depth of the plane iron to be adjusted by a knurled thumb wheel. Still later in the century came the Traut patent lever to control the lateral adjustment of the iron. These three controls, still in use on modern all-metal planes, made the wooden-bodied planes of this transitional design easy and precise to adjust and use.

I keep a set of Bailey planes, and they are a joy to use. I recommend them if you like to use wooden planes but have trouble adjusting them. The iron support and adjustment mechanism is held to the wooden body by screws that occasionally work loose. These screws must be kept tight or the iron bed will become misaligned with the wooden bed and the iron will chatter and be next to impossible to adjust.

Baileys are easy to adjust and use.

plane makes one constant cut down the entire length of the board. When you get the one unbroken shaving, the surface is either dead straight or a long gentle convex arc. Sight down the length and see what you have. If the board dips at one or both ends, it is because you have been dipping the plane. Try to use the plane as though you were attempting to make the surface concave. You won't be able to accomplish this with a plane of this length, but the attempt should counteract the end dipping.

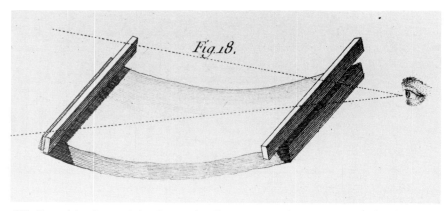

Winding sticks show twisting but not bending, as shown in this plate from Roubo.

Testing

Usually you can look down the length of a board and see how well you have leveled a surface. There are ways, though, to amplify the eye's sense of judgment. Test critical right angles by sliding a square down the length of the angle and looking for gaps between the blade of the square and the surface in question. You can test for twisting, or "winding," in a surface by setting a pair of long, perfectly true rectangular "winding sticks" on either end of the plank. The length of the sticks will exaggerate any error and make it immediately apparent to the eye.

Once a surface is true to your satisfaction, you can, by using a common marking gauge, delineate a perfectly parallel face on the other side. When this opposing face has been planed true to the gauge marks, bring one of the remaining two sides true and at right angles to the two finished surfaces. Use the gauge again to delineate the final face, plane it to the lines, and test the results with a try square. This squaring up of rough stock is one of the most basic and critical operations in planing. You do it a lot.

An iron set too rank caused this chattering. The throat of this plane is also way too open.

Problems

There are a multitude of woes that can arise to plague you in planing. The iron may chatter; the throat may clog up; the wood may splinter out ahead; a nicked or ill-set iron may leave tracks. These are all problems from setting up the plane, and there is a solution for each.

Chattering occurs when the iron repeatedly bends back and then springs forward as the plane progresses along the wood. This means that the iron is either too far extended or is not well supported behind the cutting edge. Very thin irons or narrow sharpening bevels are more prone to chattering than thicker ones. The remedy for nonsupport is either to reduce the amount of protrusion of the iron or to correct its seating in the throat. If the iron is not seated flat against its support (because of warping or ill manufacture), this defect must be corrected by shims or very cautious reshaping of the throat.

A clogged throat may also be caused by having the plane set too rank. The amount being taken off may simply be too great to clear the narrow opening. The nature of the material being planed is quite often an accessory to this difficulty, but since there is little you can do about this (except allowing green wood to season), adjustments must be made with the plane. Sometimes chronic choking can be remedied by rubbing the inside of the throat with a candle. Your technique may also be at fault. Try taking long rhythmic strokes rather than short ones. The problem may be, though, that the cap iron is set too close to the cutting edge for this particular job and is forcing the shaving into too tight a curl.

Try correcting all of these adjustments before you attempt even minor surgery on the plane. Many a plane

It's rare to see a worn moulding plane repaired with a "boxed" throat. Note the tiny dovetail keys that secure the boxwood repair piece. The lower plane is also badly worn and leaves a rough surface owing to its excessively open throat.

has been injured by cutting the throat wider to prevent choking. Another form of malpractice is using nails or metal picks to remove clogged shavings from the throat. This not only can take the edge off of the iron but it will often cut pockets in the wood of the plane or wedge that will aggravate the problem. Use only a wooden stick to clear the throat, or better yet remove the wedge and iron and correct the problem.

Splintering or tearing out ahead of the iron is a problem that often occurs when the wood is not completely dry. The wood is lifted ahead of the iron and breaks before it is severed. An iron that is set too deeply will also cause this, as will having the cap iron set too far back up from the edge. Splintering and tearing is particularly a problem with planes whose thoats are too open. As the sole of a plane wears, the throat becomes progressively wider. Some wooden planes are designed with the narrow part of the throat extending for an inch or so up into the body to maintain a constant opening as the sole is used up. Many planes, however, are not so designed or become worn beyond this point. The remedy in this case is to inset a piece of hard wood into the sole ahead of the throat to close the gap. I have seen some interesting local and regional variations in the shape of this inset piece—keystones, semicircles, plain squares—and in the materials used—from beech and ebony to brass. Metal and exotic hardwoods have a striking appearance, but since they will not wear or move with humidity changes at the same rate as the beech body of the plane, they can become just another source of trouble.

A plane that leaves track lines ("writing its name") on the wood either has a nick in the iron or is maladjusted so that the iron is sticking low in one corner. If efforts to

correct an ill-set iron are not successful, the bed of the plane is likely out of line or the iron is not ground square to its length. This can cause the throat to choke as well because an inordinate amount of shavings are forced into one corner. Test both the sole and the iron with a try square and make any necessary adjustments.

Other Angles

As a first departure from the common planes, there are those which differ in having their irons set at a pitch angle other than 45 degrees. Planes for working in very hard woods often have a pitch of 50 degrees. (Moulding planes also have a steeper pitch, up to 60 degrees.) Scraper and toothing planes have irons that are vertical or inclined slightly ahead of vertical. These are designed for finishing gnarly wood and for preparing a surface for gluing on veneer.

At the other end of the scale are the low-angle planes intended primarily for working end grain. Wooden "strike block" planes usually have their iron at a pitch of 35 degrees.

When used in conjunction with the miter-jack, this low-angle plane allows you to plane two pieces of wood to perfect, glass-smooth 45-degree angles. The back side of the miter-jack does perfect 90-degree angles.

Planes with a pitch angle at or below 20 degrees, are, of necessity, constructed of metal and have irons set in with the bevels facing up, away from the surface being worked.

Moulding Planes

Moulding planes work much the same way as bench planes, but they leave the surface in a decorative or functional profile other than flat. Moulding planes from the eighteenth century usually have strongly chamfered upper edges and a tall wedge ending in a circular outline. They may also be of nonstandard length (other than the usual 9½ inches). On later moulding planes the chamfers are less pronounced, and the finial of the wedge is swept back rather than circular in profile.

Two other features of interest on moulding planes are stamps and boxing. Wooden planes are usually stamped on their ends with the name of the manufacturer and often with that of the owner. These identifying marks are of great interest to collectors (indeed, they may be the only item of interest to some) and record the history of the tool from manufacture through the series of owners down to you. "Boxing" refers to the strips of boxwood inset into the major points of wear on the sole of the

The wedge style in the foreground is earlier than the "swept-back" style behind it.

Maker's marks, owner's marks, and boxing.

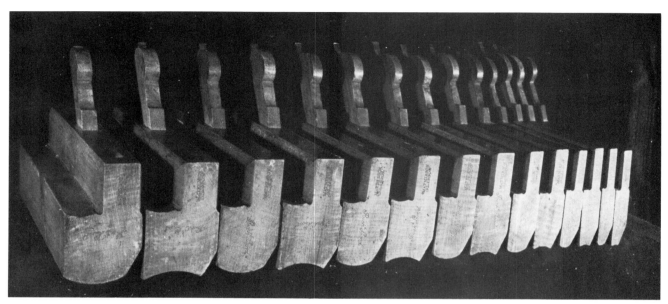

Hollows and rounds.

A bead, a reed, and an ovolo. Note the spring angle of the ovolo.

The cove plane.

plane. Box is extremely hard and long wearing. The pieces may be keyed into the beech body with a long dovetail cross-section or simply glued into long slots.

The most basic moulding planes are known as "hollows" and "rounds." These were supplied individually or in matched sets of up to thirty or more pairs graduated from $1/16$ inch up to 2 inches or so. Each "hollow" forms a convex profile on a surface; the matching "round" forms the corresponding concave profile. These hollows and rounds are quite versatile. Used individually, they can form everything from the flutes on columns to perfect round chair legs. Used in combination, the hollow and round can form more complex mouldings, particularly the wave-shaped ogee, a classic decorative moulding.

Other simple moulding planes of the hollow persuasion produce a bead on the edge of the board. When such a plane is capable of working in the middle rather than the side of a surface, it is known as a center bead. Multiple beads are reeding planes and a simple quarter round with shoulders is an ovolo.

Simple convex-bottomed planes have fewer variations. These include, most notably, those which form a cove on the edge of a board and the larger planes used for smoothing the insides of wooden rain gutters.

More complex moulding planes combine hollows, rounds, squares, and bevels to form a single unified pattern with one plane. The most common of these complex patterns is the ogee mentioned earlier. This mathematically derived S shape may be combined with beads, ovolos, and the like, to make quite sophisticated patterns.

This double-ogee crown moulding plane has a five-inch-wide iron and requires four men to pull the tow rope while one man rides the plane.

Rounder Planes

Some planes are easy to find and some are not. Fortunately, one of the most difficult to find is also one of the easiest to make. Rounder planes are quite useful for making ladder rungs, rake handles (stails), and the like. In Britain these tools are known as stail engines when used for making rake handles and as rung engines when used for making ladder rungs. Adjustable versions are known in America as witchets.

To make a single-size version (1¼ inches in diameter is useful) find a piece of seasoned hardwood, such as dogwood, maple, beech, or birch, about 9 inches long, 3 inches wide, and 2 inches thick. Locate its center on one wide face and inscribe a 1¾-inch circle around this point with a compass. Bore a 1¼-inch-diameter hole through the piece in the middle of this circle. Now, using either gouges and rasps or a cooper's tapered bung-hole borer, enlarge the hole until it meets the outer circle on one face, leaving it at its original size on the other.

To make the slot for the blade, draw a line touching the tops of the openings on both sides and parallel to the edge of the wood. You now need to know the thickness of the material from which you will make the blade. A replacement blade for a spokeshave, which is available from large hardware dealers, will do well, as will a piece of steel cut with a hacksaw from an old crosscut saw. Align this piece on one face of the wood so that its upper side crosses the line at a 30-degree angle into the circle. Scribe along its underside to mark where to cut the wood to seat the blade and then repeat this on the opposite face.

A cooper's bung borer makes the tapered hole of the rounder plane easy.

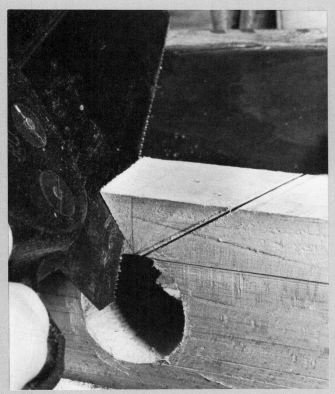

Lay out the opening for the iron and saw very carefully.　　　　*A spokeshave iron works well.*

Connect the two lines across the edge of the wood and carefully make the saw cut on the waste side of these lines. Hold the blade back in position and scribe another set of lines at right angles to the first that will leave about 1/16 inch of opening ahead of where the blade will meet the wood being rounded. The blade is held in position by two screws that pass through it into the wooden body. The holes in the blade need to be larger than the shanks of the screws to leave room for adjustment. In a scrap blade you can hacksaw and snap out slots; in a spokeshave iron it's best to drill oversized holes.

Grind the length of the blade at an angle to fit evenly into the opening; sharpen it to a 30-degree bevel and slightly round the corners. Set it on the wood bevel side down in such a way that it protrudes just a hair evenly into the length of the opening. Mark the centers of the oversized holes in the blade on the wood and prebore the pilot holes for the screws at these points. Put washers on the screws, rub their threads with candle wax, and tighten the blade into position. Try it out on a length of wood that has been roughly shaved to just fit in on the bigger side. The wood will emerge very rough if the cut is too deep, and the rounder plane will be very hard to turn if the cut is too shallow. Readjust the iron as necessary. Candle wax rubbed in the opening is a great help.

You can put handles on either end by turning the whole tool on a lathe (with the blade removed) or by cutting it down with saws and rasps. This rounder plane will follow curves in the stock being rounded very well, sometimes too well. If you leave a longer, noncutting, cylindrical passage on the trailing end of the hole, the plane will tend to follow a straighter path, just like a jointer.

Spring

Moulding planes are often designed to work at an angle tilted away from the surface that they are working. This tilted working angle is referred to as the "spring." The object is to align the iron with the average angle of the moulding being planed. Since the mouldings, with all their ins and outs, form a more or less inclined edge on the board, the plane must be inclined as well.

When working a moulding (often called "sticking"), the same general guidelines for planing apply. Usually, though, you want to start planing a short section at the far end and work your way backward down the board, finishing with a single pass down the whole length. Be sure to hold the plane at the proper spring angle and bear with your left hand into the board from the side as you propel and push down with your right. Most edge-working moulding planes have a noncutting extension on the left-hand side of the sole which acts as a fence. This fence needs to ride against the outer edge as the plane works downward. Most moulding planes cannot be turned around and worked from the other direction on the same edge of the board when the grain of the wood is troublesome. It is best to select straight-grained stock with the growth rings oriented at right angles to the edge of the plane iron. Dry, quarter-sawn stock planes best.

Tongue and Groove, Rabbets, and Dados

Making a groove down the length of a board calls for a plane with an iron equal in width to the groove you want and some sort of "fence" arrangement to ride along the edge of the

The homemade grooving plane at top has an iron made from an old file. Two tonguing planes wait on the bench; one has a fence adjustable by screw arms, the other by wedges.

The skew-iron rabbet plane.

This filletster has a skew iron, an edge nicker, a fence, and a depth stop and can cut cross-grain smooth as glass.

The dado plane has stops, nickers, and a skewed iron, but no fence.

board and keep the groove properly aligned. A simple grooving plane may have but a single iron and a fixed fence. More versatile grooving planes, such as the plow plane, can take irons of different widths and have adjustable fences that move on arms. When you plane a groove, start at the far end of the board and work your way back. A grooving plane is usually equipped with a depth stop of some sort; so just work until the plane "bottoms out," step backward, and do the next section until you have done the whole length.

Tonguing planes are the opposite of grooving planes. They have a gap in the middle of the iron that removes the wood on either side and leaves the tongue in the middle. Like grooving planes, they may have either a fixed or a movable fence. If you do not possess a tonguing plane, you can use a plow to cut away the wood on both sides of where you want the tongue to be. It takes twice as long, but it works in a pinch. Often tongue and groove planes are combined as one plane or made in sets. These are referred to as "match" planes, and tongue and groove boards are commonly referred to as "matched" boards.

Rabbets are shoulders or steps cut into the side of a board. A rabbet plane must have its iron slightly greater than the width of the bed of the plane so that it can reach right up flush on the sides. A simple rabbet has no fence to guide it parallel to the established edge, relying instead on your left hand hanging under the bed to hold it at a constant distance. Your fingers are the fence.

A more sophisticated rabbet plane equipped with an adjustable fence and depth stop is better known as a filletster. The fence may be held either by screws to the sole of the plane or with arms similar to the plow plane and will reveal only as much of the iron as

The old woman's tooth.

The "universal" plane and some of the planes it replaced.

needed. A variation on the filletster is the sash filletster used for cutting the glazing rabbets when marking window sash. The fence on a sash filletster will not slide over and cover the iron because it is intended to ride against the moulded side of the sash bar while the plane cuts the rabbet on the opposite side.

Rabbet planes enter a different world in planing in that they are sometimes employed to cut across rather than along the grain. A common plane with its mouth set at right angles to the length of the plane body will work across the grain, but the resulting surface is often rough and coarse. The roughness results from having the iron approach the fibers broadside so that they are torn out before they are sliced. The solution is to have the iron and throat of the plane set in at a skewed angle to the direction of the thrust of the plane. This skew iron severs only part of a longitudinal fiber at a time and can cut across the grain as smooth as glass. You can see how this functions by taking a regular plane and trying it first straight across the grain and then with the body held at an angle to the thrust. The angled thrust should leave a much smoother surface, but you will quickly notice how the throat of a regular plane chokes in the trailing corner. The plane needs to be designed for skew cutting to do it well.

Another design feature sometimes found on skew-mouth or other planes for cutting across the grain is a vertical knife to sever the grain at the edge of the cut before the plane reaches it. This precutting results in a sharply defined shoulder. Otherwise the corner of iron would tear and splinter the wood. These knives are usually retractable or removable for circumstances where their services are not required. To form a sharp shoulder across the grain with a plane lacking an integral knife requires a separate knife and a straight edge. Compare this knife and plane combination to the raker-tooth crosscut saws in the previous chapter. Same job, same action.

A dado is a groove made across a board. Planes designed specifically for this job are equipped with scoring knives on both sides of the body to precede the skewed cutting iron. A fence would not be effective over the great distance required to reach the nearest parallel surface, so instead a guide board is clamped to the wood itself.

Another plane used in dado work is the router plane. In wooden versions it is known somewhat unkindly as an "old woman's tooth." When the dado has been roughed out by sawing the sides and chiseling out the bottom, the router plane is set to the required depth to finish the job. Router planes are quite versatile and can be used to cut a recessed field of constant depth or a groove parallel to a curved edge.

As you can see, the abilities granted you by woodworking planes are myriad. They are elegant and individualistic creations in themselves, attractive items to own and use. I can't talk about planes in general, though, without mentioning the "universal" planes that so fulfilled the Victorian ideal of a tool that could do everything. Virtually a planing mill in your hand, these planes could replace a whole chest of wooden planes, as indeed they did. Younger joiners began to take them up, though, just as the use of hand-planed mouldings began to yield to the pressure of cheaper stock coming from centralized mill-work shops. These planes closed out an era.

THE SASH JOINER

Of the making of windows, there is no end.

Windowmaking (1930)

A hole in the side of your hut that is not your door is a wind-eye. When you put vertical bars in the wind-eye to keep the wolves out, you have mullions. When you add horizontal bars to reinforce the verticals, you find the rain hanging in drops from them and blowing into your room. So you put the crossed bars in diagonally, and now the rain runs to the sides of the frame and off the slanting window-sill. When it gets so that you can afford to buy glass to fill in between the diagonals, you let in the light, but now you keep out the air. The only experience that you have with things that open and close is with doors and shutters. Following suit, you make your windows to swing open to the side as hinged casements. Finally, as a dedicated follower of fashion, you succumb to the new style of having vertically sliding sash windows with rectangular panes. Not wanting to hoist lead windows, you make the sash of wood and use the lead as a counterweight. Whew!

You have been looking *through* windows all your life, but have you ever looked *at* one? On the surface, there is little variation between most windows. Beneath the paint, however, the design and process of the joinery is much more varied than one might expect. Sash joinery has long been a specialty trade in woodworking. A person who would think nothing of building his own home would still probably buy his windows ready-made. In leaving the windows to a specialist, he would be following the practice of many centuries.

In fact, there is no reason for every man jack to possess the special tools and skills necessary for window making. Windows can be done more easily and cheaply in a shop that is set up for just such a purpose. Window joinery, though, is a skill that one can learn— and a useful one at that. There are many ways to work and many win-

Muntins from an eighteenth-century sash.

An eighteenth-century muntin (left) and a nineteenth-century muntin (right).

dows to make for houses and furniture as well.

The basic window sash is a rectangular frame of four sticks: two vertical "stiles" and a top and bottom "rail." The space within the frame is divided into smaller rectangles by narrower sticks called "muntins" or "sash bars." The individual sticks have seats, or "rabbets," planed into one face to take the glazing and are moulded on the other face to reduce their obtrusiveness but not their strength. These sticks are held together with mortice and tenon joints that vary in design and placement according to the way the window is hung, the tools available, and the training of the joiner.

A study of the evolution of technique in woodworking, particularly in its practical applications, reveals the adaptability that has enabled the craftsman and his children to survive. At times the economic environment permits him to develop his craftsmanship to great heights; at other times he can barely hold his own. Looking at sash through two centuries, one can follow the joiner's response to the increasing demand for cheaper and more plentiful goods and the growing competition from mechanized production.

Georgian Sash

Every eighteenth-century window sash that I have seen has muntins moulded with inset quarter-rounds called "ovolos" that are about as fat as they are deep. The stiles are continuous from top to bottom, and the horizontal rails are tenoned into them. The upright muntins are tenoned into the top and bottom rails. The cross muntins are the shortest pieces, tenoned into the stiles and the upright muntins.

Dimensions

Windows may either be made in standard dimensions or custom made to fit a particular opening. Often the sizes of glass available determine the dimensions. The stock is generally 1 inch thick for all pieces. The bottom rail is the widest piece, 1½ to 2½ inches, while the stiles are a bit narrower and the top rail is equal in width to the stiles or as narrow as an inch if it is the meeting rail in double-hung sash. The top, or meeting, rail in double-hung sash is made narrow to prevent it from being obtrusive. Ob-

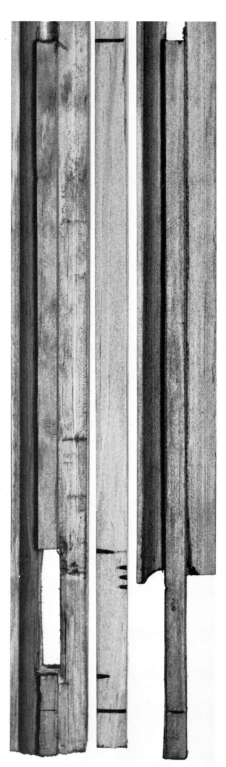

The vertical guide stick flanked by a stile (left) and an upright muntin (right). All work has been completed except for sawing off the "horns" at the bottoms.

viously, the bottom rail of the top sash in double-hung windows is a meeting rail as well and must be made to the same dimensions. In earlier double-hung windows only the bottom sash was movable; the top was fixed.

Guide Sticks

Since you will often be making more than one window of a given size and pattern, much time and trouble can be saved by making a pair of guide sticks for laying out both the vertical and horizontal pieces. Because each mortice and tenon joint is a complicated arrangement with multiple shoulders, correctly making and using these guide sticks is critical to your success.

The vertical guide stick is used to lay out both the stiles and the upright muntins simultaneously. These measurements are best kept separate by marking one edge of the guide stick for the muntins and one edge for the stiles. The markings for the stile need to show, from the bottom up, the starting point; the beginning and end of the mortice to take the tenon on the bottom rail; the beginning and end of the mortice for each cross muntin;

the mortice to take the top rail; and the end point. Remember that none of these points will correspond to the actual glass panes that you will use but, depending on how you are working, are either determining or determined by the size of the panes.

The upright muntins have tenons on either end and require different marking. The guide marks for them must show, again from the bottom up, the starting point; the lower shoulder of the ovolo on the interior of the bottom rail; the shoulder of the glazing rabbet on the exterior of the bottom rail; and the upper edge of the ovolo on the bottom rail. The next set of marks shows where to cut the mortice to take the first cross muntin. This set of marks is the same as those marked on the stiles since the cross muntin intersects both at the same height. The marks for the cross muntins for both the stiles and the upright muntins continue to correspond on the guide stick until you reach the top rail, where the procedure for the bottom is followed in reverse order.

The marks on the guide stick for the vertical members began and ended differently for the stiles and upright muntins, but were the same for both of them in the middle. The

marks for the horizontal members are just the opposite: the marks for the rails and the cross muntins are the same on either end but different in the middle. Both the rails and the cross muntins are tenoned on their extreme ends. In their midsections, however, at the same points where the rails are morticed to take the uprights, the cross muntins are sawn through and tenoned. The marks on the horizontal guide stick, then, must indicate the three-shouldered tenon-cutting sequence at either end, marks which are shared by both the rails and the cross muntins. The midsection, where the joints with the upright muntins are made, must show tenon-cutting sequences for the cross muntins and morticing sequences for the rails. These various midsection marks are based on a common centerline.

Since the measurements for the tenon-cutting sequence are dependent on the profile cut by your moulding plane, you had better first try the plane and see just what that profile is. It may take you some practice to get consistent results, and for the window to come out right, the mouldings must be consistent. In one respect, then, it would be easier to plane all the pieces with their rabbets and ovolos and

The horizontal guide stick with the bottom rail (below) and a crossbar (above). The crossbar has not yet been separated and scribed.

then measure and cut all the joints. The problem with this is that the mouldings get bunged up during the process of cutting the joints.

The best compromise is to mark all the pieces while they are still square and unmoulded. Chop all of the mortices but saw just the shoulders of the tenons. Both the mortices and the tenons are laid out with the guide sticks and a double-toothed morticing gauge. This gauge is of course set to mark lines equal in width and placement to the fillet (the square shoulder) between the ovolo and the rabbet. The width of this fillet in turn must be made to correspond to the width of the appropriate morticing chisel, usually ¼ or ⅜ inch.

Well-seasoned stock with straight, even grain is best for window making. Lightness, stability, strength, and ease of working are all important. Oak was used in the earliest sash, but was rapidly superseded by "softwoods," such as white or yellow pine. As usual, try and orient the growth rings of the wood perpendicular to the major surfaces of the geometrical section. Proper orientation minimizes distortion and windows that stick in the summertime.

Before going any further, mark all of your pieces so that you can maintain them in the same up-and-down, left-and-right order in which they were laid out. Use a pencil and mark them in a place that will not be planed away. Out-of-order or inverted muntins cause crooked windows.

So, mark all of the pieces, saw the tenon shoulders, and chop the mortices through, half from one side and half from the other. The mortices in the sides of the stiles for the cross muntins need go in only a short ways, as they will not be pegged. The stiles are morticed near their ends and need to be left about an inch longer than necessary on both ends to leave "horns" that will strengthen the ends

during morticing. They will be sawn off after final assembly.

Moulding

The cross-section of a standard eighteenth-century muntin is created by attacking the four corners of the inch-square stock with planes. The rabbets are planed into the exterior (outside of the house) corners. The typical inset quarter rounds or Roman ovolos are planed into the interior corners. Holding the narrow muntins during planing can be a nuisance; so joiners who do a lot of sash work make themselves a special cradle called a sticking board.

The sticking board has shoulders and grooves along its length to seat the muntin firmly for each of the four steps in planing. The far end of the muntin being planed butts up against a fixed stop (a protruding screw head) on the end of the sticking board. As the muntins vary in length, they are held on the near end by driving a small blade called a bench knife into the surface of the sticking board and the end of the muntin. The stiles and rails are rabbeted and moulded on one face only and are large enough to plane directly on the bench using either the end vise or the bench stop and holdfast.

When all of the pieces have been fully moulded, all that remains is to finish the tenons and assemble the window. If these were simple tenons, all you would have to do would be to saw or split down the cheeks to the previously sawn shoulder. On the rabbeted side indeed that is it. On the moulded ovolo side, though, you need to cut away enough of the ovolo on the tenoned piece exactly to fit over the ovolo on the morticed piece.

This is referred to as "scribing." It is superior to a butt miter, where the two pieces are cut at 45 degrees, in

that it will not open up and show a crack. When this sort of scribed joint is viewed straight from the face side of the window, the junction line appears to be a simple 45-degree angle, as indeed it is, for mitering the ovolo is the first step in scribing the joint.

Using a miter template of beech or brass to guide the chisel, slice the end of the ovolo to a perfect 45 degrees. Do both sides of the muntin tenons and the one side of the rail tenons. Now, turn these mitered tenons sideways and undercut them by first continuing the cheek of the tenon to the base of the miter with a saw and then paring out the remainder by pushing in from both sides with an in-cannel (beveled on the concave side) gouge. When used for this purpose, these gouges are known as scribing gouges and are matched to the radius of the ovolo on your plane.

Before assembling any of the pieces, bore the holes for the pegs through the cheeks of the mortices in the stiles. Push the pieces together, see that they are cleanly seated, and mark the location of the peg holes on the cheeks of the tenons. Pull the joints apart and bore the peg holes through the tenons so that they are offset ¹⁄₁₆ inch toward the tenon shoulder. Split out pegs from the waste sawn off the cheeks of the tenons, point their ends, and drive them in. The offsetting of the hole in the tenon from the holes through the mortice will cause the joint to be drawn up tight as a tick.

Victorian Sash

After 1800 the way of window making started to change. The muntins became narrower in width but deeper on the rabbeted face. New tools became available which made the moulding process easier and more accessible. I have often encountered

Lay out the mortices and tenons with the guide sticks and morticing gauge. Chop the mortices, but saw only the shoulders of the tenons.

Cut the first rabbet in the sawn and morticed muntins with a panel plow or sash filletster plane while it is held in the sticking board.

a type of mid-Victorian sash joinery practiced in our county which runs counter to the practice of the previous century. The houses in which I have found these sash all have nice looking exteriors but generally shoddy framework. Life was not easy in the post-war South. I have had occasion to repair and replace sash from this period and, not to try and "improve" on historical evidence, have attempted to follow their ways of working as closely as possible.

The first difference is in the mould-ing of the stock. Instead of using the two separate planes, the sash ovolo plane and the rabbet plane, the two planes are combined by fastening them together with screws and pegs. This allows you to cut the ovolo and the rabbet simultaneously and quite accurately and consistently. The cross-section of the muntin is much narrower than before, and the shoulder of the glazing rabbet and the shoulder of the ovolo are now in line with one another rather than offset. This makes layout easier than it was

when every tenon had three shoulders that had to be marked. Using a plane that cuts both features of the moulding at once also eliminates the need for the sticking board. Instead of being planed out one at a time, the muntins are planed out double, as back-to-back Siamese twins. This makes them large enough to hold in the end vise or with a bench stop and holdfast. When the planing is done, the two muntins are separated by running a cutting gauge down their middle and snapping them apart.

Set the muntin in its second position on the sticking board and cut the second rabbet.

With the muntin in its third position, plane the first ovolo.

Flip the muntin into its fourth position and finish the moulding.

Finish sawing the cheeks of the tenons slightly down below the shoulder. This is a rail and hence is moulded and rabbeted only on one side.

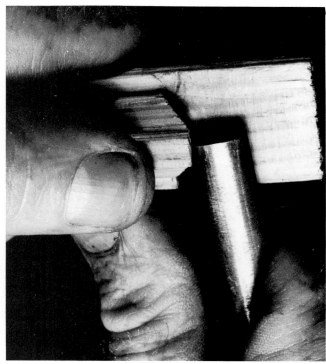

Slice off the ovolos at a 45-degree angle.

Complete the tenon by scribing with an in-cannel gouge.

The lower left corners of a Georgian sash (left) and a Victorian sash (right).

The upper right corner of a Georgian sash. The notch on the right side of the stile is for a catch to hold the window open.

Moulding muntins with a double-sash plane.

The morticing machine replaces the mallet and chisel.

Once the stiles and rails are moulded, they are laid out with guide sticks as before, but here another difference arises. In most window sash the stiles go from top to bottom with the rails set in between them. In these, however, the top rail extends the full width of the window and the stiles are truncated. The bottom rail is made in the normal manner.

If the joiner had been trying to make the window weather tight, this arrangement would make sense. Since the top rail of the lower sash and the bottom rail of the upper sash overlap, they can be shaped so as to wedge against one another and form a

tighter seal. A continuous top rail makes this much easier to accomplish. In all of the windows that I have seen made in this manner, however, the top rail is rectangular in cross-section with no hint of a wedge shape to act as a weather seal.

I sometimes get the feeling from these windows that the joiner was attempting to replicate machine work by hand. In scribing muntins, for example, rather than strike a miter and pare out the waste with a gouge as outlined earlier, he apparently used a profile template on the side of the muntin and removed the waste with a coping saw. This way of working en-

tirely from the side is how the job would be approached by someone using a high-speed rotary shaper. A similar but earlier tack was to run a special coping plane down the end grain of all the tenoned stock. Neither of these methods requires that the stock be premoulded. Such treatment, in fact, would leave the back edge of the ovolo prone to splintering during planing.

Even though many windows of this genre show coping saw work on the muntins, all have some gouge work in the joints between stile and rail. It is in these most important joints that the integrity of the sash appears to be

Coping the muntin.

The upper left corner of local Victorian sash.

compromised. The best practice is to scribe along the whole length of the shoulder of a tenoned piece to cup over and interlock with the ovolo on the morticed piece. A faster and cheaper practice is simply to slice off the moulding on the face of the mor- ticed piece, leaving only a quarter inch or so of the ovolo to keep up appearances. The ovolo on the ten- oned piece is scribed back only as much as is necessary to house the little piece left on the mortice face. The resulting joint suffers mainly in its resistance to warping and twisting, which admittedly is not as important a factor in framed sliding sash as it

would be in free-swinging casements. In resistance to tension failure, which is the way sliding sash is going to come apart, this joint is as strong as the other.

Whatever sort of sash you make, when it comes time to glaze it, you can even make the putty yourself from powdered chalk or shell and linseed oil. The glass can be first secured by tapping tiny snipped brads into the sides of the rabbet with the edge of the putty knife slid flat against the pane. The white putty on the wide muntins and shallow rabbets of eighteenth-century sash gives those windows a prominence and solidity

that was deliberately minimized in the later tendency toward narrower mun- tins and ever-larger panes.

RIVEN ROOF

Clapboards . . . hewing and nailing them on roofes
and sides of houses, well done not worth above
5 shillings per hundred, butt as most are done, not worth
above 2 shillings 6 pence

wage and price regulations, General Court of New Haven (1640)

*A cypress shingle roof going on near our
carpenter's shop at Colonial Williamsburg.*

Folks just off the boat in the 1600s had to make a number of fast changes in their thinking to get a roof over their heads. They were coming from a land of stone, tile, and thatch, from a land of gentle rains to one of tropical downpours. Many arrived totally unprepared to meet their most basic needs. They came without the physical or mental tools needed in the New World.

The native population had of course long been adapted to the materials and climate of North America. Even without metal tools they fashioned weather-tight dwellings from reed mats and bark.

Many trees, the tulip poplar in particular, yield great sheets of half-inch-thick waterproof building material as big as two men can handle. The bark is a good insulator, is waterproof (if it weren't, the tree would dry out and die), and will last for years. Tulip poplars grow straight and cylindrical so the harvested bark lies smooth and flat. In the spring, when the tree is growing fast, the layer of cells between the bark and the wood is very fragile and easily broken. The traditional expression of this is, "The bark comes off easy when the sap is rising."

I sat out many a deluge under a bark roof the first year that I moved to Virginia. We were cutting poplars to make weatherboards, and as it was mid-May, we had only to slit the bark down the length of the fresh-cut log, work the edges loose with the edge of our axes and peel it back, just like taking a jacket off a drunk. When the bark is loose all the way around, a strong kick on one end will dislodge the slick white log and it will slide free from the bark envelope as if there were no friction at all. It is quite a pleasure to see a heavy log move with such incredible ease.

Once the bark is free from the log,

it can be laid out flat and weighted down so it cannot curl into a tight roll as it will want to do. When they dry, the flat sheets will still tend to curl a bit in the weather unless they are well fastened on the walls and roof. Poplar bark still covers many a house in the Eastern mountains, and in Canada huge barns grow old under roofs of elm bark shingles.

The process of splitting wood to make thin pieces to use for house coverings was well known for centuries before the bounty of the New World was harvested. The term *clapboard* which we now use to refer to any tapered siding, at one time exclusively meant split oak that had been imported into England from northern Germany for the manufacture of barrel staves. The oak was worked by cleaving rather than sawing not only because it was easier and faster but because the resulting product was stronger and more durable. In splitting wood one follows the path of least resistance down the length of the grain, a path that sawing would ignore. Since the split follows the grain, riven wood is both less permeable and less prone to breakage.

Just as the coopers were interested in cleft oak for keeping water in, house builders were interested in it for keeping water out. The second definition of the word *clapboard* is thin, tapered, "feather-edged" boards lapped horizontally for the covering of a house. This second definition is primarily an American one and has been applied, perhaps incorrectly, to every early American usage of the word.

In his 1684 tract "Information and Direction to Such Persons as are inclined to America," William Penn makes moderately clear the distinction between the two uses of the word when he describes the construction of a house that can be built by

"ordinary beginners." "For Covering the House, Ends, and Sides, and for the Loft, we use *Clabboard*, which is *Rived feather-edged*, of five foot and half long, that well Drawn, lyes close and smooth." He goes on to say that "the lower flour is the *Ground*, the upper Clabboard." The shapes and dimensions of timber suitable for exterior siding are not the same as those of wood used for flooring. The careful qualifier added to his first use of the word shows the difference and a meaning in transition.

Building with riven stock has the advantage of requiring only minimal equipment. An early apprenticeship record states that the master shall provide the apprentice on completion of his term the necessary tools to build a "clapboard house." Since a clapboard house can be built without any sawn stock at all, the master is spared the considerable expense of supplying a pit saw for making plank. Basically his obligation is limited to a hammer, a chisel, an auger, an axe, and a froe. These in exchange for seven years' labor.

Just about any wood that will split straight will make good shingles or clapboards. Some species are certainly more naturally durable than others, but even the most decay-prone woods will last for decades if properly riven and laid. A multitude of factors determine how long a given roof will last, all bearing on how well the roof sheds water and dries out. Wood will not rot unless it stays damp.

Red oak, a common material for shingle and clapboard making, shows this principle best of all. Unlike the white oak species, red oaks do not develop "tyloses," or blocks in the vessels formed every spring, and thus they remain porous from end to end. The slower the tree grows, the closer together are these rings of vessels and the more porous the wood. Yet as porous as the wood is from end to end, it is still relatively impermeable across its grain.

Since the splitting follows the grain of the oak from end to end, the exposed surface is made up of the tiny tubes torn open down their whole length. This leaves a surface of a million tiny rain gutters that shed water as though off the back of the proverbial duck. Many folks like to shave shingles to a taper and a smooth surface. If you were to do this to a riven red-oak shingle, you would cut into the pores of the wood, open the grain, and allow it to become saturated with water, and it would rot in no time. Sawn shingles are just as bad or worse. Keep the rough split to the weather at all times in any sort of wood.

A feather-edged clapboard roof.

Board Trees

For floors, roofs, walls, or barrels, riven stock begins with finding the tree. You're looking for clear, straight-grained wood as large and long as you can find. For the first Europeans arriving on the new continent, this caliber of tree was certainly more abundant than it was back in the Old World. But even with the vast forests, the difficulty of transporting timber from any great distance necessitated early legislation (in Plymouth colony as soon as six years after settlement) against the profligate use or export of timber suitable for riving.

Some communities were better off than others in their proximity to timber supplies, but since it takes about a century for a tree to get big enough to rive cleanly, this resource is only occasionally renewable when man is about. Not long after settlement, good shingle trees could be found only in the deep recesses of the for-

A shaved red oak shingle (above) and an unshaved red oak shingle (below). When they are submerged in water and air is blown through their ends, the difference in surface porosity is evident.

est, where the profit margin for the loggers shrank.

I have worked with trees from this time, old survivors that finally went down in a storm, huge oaks from deep in the forest. From them it was possible to rive clean, 6 feet long and a foot wide, straight as an arrow. In

A good white oak board tree.

Breaking short bolts from a good red oak.

an afternoon's work one 6-foot length yielded enough clapboards to cover the wall of a house. Would that there were more.

It seems a bit odd, but now the best trees come not from the wild forest beyond the reach of man but from domestic trees that have been deliberately saved to shade houses, parks, and churchyards. Their branches may begin lower than forest trees, and they may contain the occasional railroad spike or ingrown horseshoe, but they can be of prodigious breadth. When a tree of this size goes down, it is often too big for the firewood cutters, and if you hear about it in time, you can get ahold of it

before they do something drastic and destroy it for more appropriate uses.

You usually have to cut a tree of this size to the lengths that you want before you can move it. You may want to split it into pieces small enough to carry on your shoulder, or you may find it easier to move by rolling if you don't have too far to go. One fellow told me that his granddaddy logged poplars in the mountains that were so big that he could cut them into 16-foot lengths and they would roll as good one way as they would the other, just like a ball. Lengths of the size trees you are likely to encounter today, however, tend to roll only in a straight line; to turn a big log roll it up onto a

chunk of wood at its balance point and pivot it to head in the new direction.

Riving

With the log back at the workplace, start the first split along one corner of the cylinder and run it along by adding wedges until the log falls in two. The very heart of the log will still be as knotty and disorganized as it was when the tree was a sapling, and you may need to use an axe to sever any crossed fibers. This problem will diminish as the work progresses. In oaks you want to continue the radial

Continue the splitting with a froe and a maul.

splitting (from heart to bark, like the spokes of a wheel) all the way down to the finished product. The process is simply to continue splitting each half in half, again and again, until the pieces reach their final dimensions.

As the pieces get smaller, they will begin to bend as they are split. A split will tend to follow the path of least resistance, which is straight down the grain, unless some other force directs its progress. If a split is begun off center, the thinner side will be bent more and the split will begin to drift to that side. You can see a model of this effect by tearing a plain sheet of paper. Start the tear in the middle and, keeping your fingers spaced equally apart, continue the tear down the middle of the paper. Now tear this half in half and so on. This is no problem as long as you keep the two pieces equal. But now try to tear a shingle-sized piece off of the side of the paper without making a corrective repositioning of your hands. It can't be done, in paper or in wood. You must either compensate for this tendency or use it to your advantage.

All of the splitting is accomplished with the froe, the maul, and a big forked limb called a riving break. This last implement allows the judicious application of leverage to correct and control the direction of the splits. If a split starts to run out, you place the thicker side down in the break and put your weight on it to overbend it as you work the froe along. To free the froe enough to move it on down, you may need to place either the handle of your maul or your free hand in the crack to hold it open.

Unlike oak and poplar, pine and cypress are only initially split radially to get them to the proper width for the final tangential splitting parallel to the growth rings. Although I still split cypress in half and in half again and so on (I'm too used to oak), some people rive cypress shingles off the edge of

Riving clapboards with the riving break.

the billet. The resulting run-out gives the shingles a lengthwise taper. As each shingle is peeled off, they invert the billet and split from the other end to keep it all even.

Radial splitting will yield wedge-shaped clapboards, which is of course exactly right for the job. Tapered lap siding lies flatter and tighter against the studs. Any sapwood, the lighter colored wood just below the bark, must be removed, since it decays quickly when exposed to the weather.

The fastest way of "sapping" is to lay the piece across a chopping block and use a hatchet to chop and split right down along the grain on the dividing line. Attempts to split off the narrow width of sapwood with a froe are usually defeated by run-out. Sometimes, however, you may find it preferable to remove the sapwood before the final riving. Since a double or quadruple thickness of sapwood can be tough to split off with a hatchet, it's better to attack the sapwood with a froe from both ends of the piece and use the hatchet only to chop off what remains.

Clapboards need a bit more shaping once they are free of sapwood. The lower, thicker edge can be draw-knifed straight and then chamfered on the outside corner to give a rain return. The upper, thinner edge will be covered by the next clapboard above so there is no need to work on it at all.

Remove all lighter-colored sapwood.

Clapboard Roofs

The very best clapboards are only six feet long. A structure of any size then will have a lot of end joints. Clapboards are typically end jointed with tapered laps. The breaks are of course arranged to happen over a rafter, but rather than butt the two boards end to end and use two nails to fasten them down, you chop away the last three inches of both boards in a taper so that they can overlap each other for that distance. They are fastened by a single nail driven through both pieces. More often than not, the joints are made all in a vertical line down every other rafter.

Clapboarding for roofs was an early solution, and not a particularly enduring one. Where clapboard roofs have survived, they have usually been saved by the addition of another wing to the building, the new roof protecting the older one. Crawling into these hot, hidden spaces to examine these roofs, one feels like Lord Carnarvan in the Valley of the Kings. The bone dry, dusty slopes of red oak still show traces of painting with pine tar, and the marks left by nicks in the cutting edge of the adze or hatchet are as plain as the day they were made.

Shingle Roofs

While a clapboard roof can be fastened directly to the rafters, shingles require the addition of horizontal "roofers" or "nailers," usually of 1-by-3-inch shingle lath. The first step is to determine the lap of the shingles. Usually a bit less than one-third of a shingle is exposed to the weather; the remaining two-thirds are covered by the shingles above. This makes three "waters" and means that at any point the roof is three shingles thick. With shingles 25 inches long, for example, 8 inches would be exposed to the weather and the nailers would be spaced at 8-inch intervals.

Working on narrow laths has two advantages. First, they act as guidelines for laying the courses of shingles straight without the need for snapping chalk lines or gauging up from the course below. Second, they afford the shingles some ventilation on their undersides. This is important in the warm wet weather that is so conducive to decay. The laths are sawn out and when they are shorter than the length of the roof, as is usually the case, they must be lapped on a rafter just as the clapboards were when they run out. This is about my favorite occupation, balanced 30 feet up on a steep-pitched lattice-work roof, adzing away the free end of the lath. You hold the end of the lath down with your toe and adze the clear pine away in a perfect bevel.

Chop the clapboard lap with a hand axe or adze.

Laying shingle lath using the poll of the adze as a hammer.

The Kick

A shingle roof is laid in sequence from the bottom up, starting at the eaves and ending at the ridge. Commonly the bottom run of shingle lath is furred up into what is termed the "kick." It is necessary because the bottom course of shingles must be doubled. If the bottom lath were not furred up, this double course would not lie at a convenient angle for adding the following courses of shingles up the roof. The shingles of the starter course need to overhang their supporting woodwork by about two inches. This means that the spacing for the first pair of laths must be two inches narrower than that for succeeding courses. To keep the overhang of the first course of shingles even, secure a string line to use as a guide at the appropriate distance.

Spacing and Nailing

Shingles need room to move as they are alternately soaked and parched by the weather. If you are nailing up green shingles, they can be butted right up against each other, for they are as wide as they are going to get. Dry, seasoned shingles need to be spaced about a quarter of an inch apart. Any closer and, when they get wet and swell, they will push against each other, buckle, and pull loose. Shingles over 8 inches wide will really do some moving; they are best split in half and nailed as two.

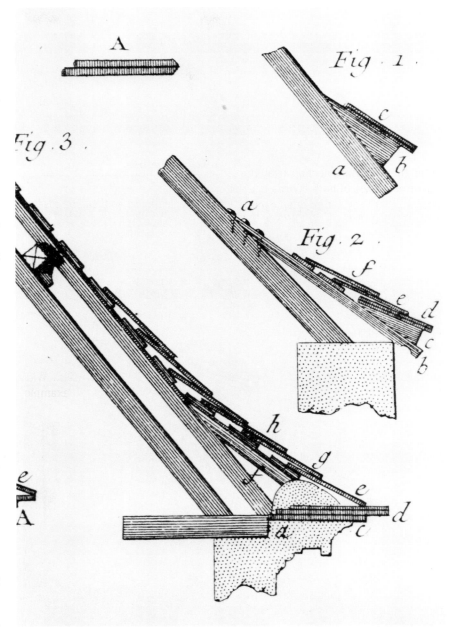

"Kicks" on tile roofs from Diderot.

I always use one nail in each shingle, placed off center where the shingle crosses the second lath down from the top. This placement in fact results in two nails through each shingle, as the nailing for the next course passes through the top ends of the shingles beneath it. The nails are offset from in off the centerline of the shingle so that they will not coincide with the gap between the shingles of the next course. The gap between any two adjoining shingles must be situated so as to be offset at least 1½ inches from the gap between the shingles beneath it.

Nailing through thin wooden shingles without cracking them requires some technique on the part both of the nail smith and of the roofer. Proper nails make the job a lot easier. Cut nails, which are flat on their points, punch through the wood, rather than push it aside as the tapered points of wire nails do; so they are much less likely to cause splits.

A cut nail has two parallel sides and

The chisel point of the hand-wrought nail must go in across the grain.

two converging sides. When driven in, the nail must be oriented so that the converging sides are facing the top and bottom of the shingle. This will direct the pressure along the grain, up and down the shingle, rather than across the grain where a split would occur. Wire nails can be blunted by standing them on their heads and hitting their points with the face of the hammer, but this gets right tedious when you have to do it several thousand times.

Most all the roofs I do now are for Colonial buildings of the pre–cut nail era. Consequently, the only appropriate nails are those handwrought by the blacksmith. These can be as difficult as wire nails to drive without causing a split, and you can't really hammer blunt the head of a handwrought nail. Instead, you or the smith can flatten the side of the point into a spade shape. This chisellike tip

Perhaps the first man who made round-bottom shingles knew that they shed water better than square bottoms, but as soon as he did it, everybody had to have them.

Another way of laying shingles in double-thick courses at my Uncle George's farm.

nailed down, with no shingle to cover the nail heads, the elements would quickly corrode the fasteners and begin the end of the roof. For this reason the last ridge courses are commonly held with pegs.

This is particularly important in coastal regions, where the salt air eats the nails out of the wood in no time. I have heard tales of shingle roofs out on the Eastern Shore that were entirely pegged. The men bored the holes with gimlets and set the pegs in with their teeth before driving them home.

Near my shop is a house that has the ridge combed in the opposite direction from every other house around. Perhaps there was a freak storm when this roof went on; for nine storms out of ten it's pointing in the wrong direction. On the tenth storm, though, this roof does just fine.

will sever the cross grain and direct the pressure up and down, rather than across the shingle. It's either this or preboring every nail hole with a gimlet.

Each succeeding course moves up the roof, guided by the laths, gauges, or chalk lines snapped on the preceding course. The lines can be snapped two at a time, as you can see the second one through the spaces between the first course of shingles.

Combing

To finish up, the ridge course on the side from which the storms come needs to extend up over the down-storm course by an inch and a half. Because these shingles are the last applied, their entire surface is exposed to the weather. If they are

Combing on the ridge seen from the down-storm side.

PITMAN'S PROGRESS

The cause of the intemperance of the sawyers, say my
informants, was their extreemly hard labour, and the thurst
produced by their great exertion.

Henry Mayhew, *London Labour and the London Poor* (1860)

It's a rare music you hear, shuffling ankle deep in fresh sawdust, elbows sweeping scant inches from the tarred plank walls of the sawpit. With each downward stroke the chorus of teeth on the 7-foot-long steel blade rips another half inch along the length of the log. The foot-thick log above your head and the walls of the pit exclude the noise and distraction of the town. There is only the relentless progression of the blade down the charcoal-struck line. Granted, pit sawing is not everyone's idea of a good time. But such labor has a transcendental quality that is as much a part of it as the sweat and fatigue and the ever-growing stack of finished lumber.

The sawyer is to the builder as the spinner is to the weaver. Early on, the waste that the axe made in reducing to chips all but the needed thickness of the log and the growing scarcity and limited species of woods that would satisfactorily yield to the wedge made the two-man rip saw essential. With such a tool two men can reduce even the most intractable elm log into a score of inch-thick coffin boards in a matter of hours. The feather-edged, tapered weather-board siding for a medium-sized house can be got out in four days sawing of one good tree.

Most all two-man ripping of lumber from logs is done in the vertical plane. You only have to think about the difficulties of doing it horizontally to see why. First, the kerf would tend to close up and pinch the saw. Second, gravity would try to pull the saw off course. With the saw vertical the man down below can use his weight to its greatest effect. The saw cuts on the downstroke, and one usually needs all the help he can get.

Although nearly a millennium has passed since the pitman was first replaced by the water wheel and the crank mechanism that now bears his name, pit saws and sawyers are still

Two pitmen at work on alternate kerfs of the same log.

at work. Sawyers at their best are specialists; never felling or carting timber, never working as carpenters, they just saw boards, which is quite enough.

Traditionally, the top sawyer was the senior of the two, owner of the saw and caretaker of its sharpness. In our yard one works in the pit or on top as the mood beckons. New men always start out in the pit simply because the motion there is more customary and easier to get used to. The pull stroke of the pitman does the actual cutting of the wood, but he is able to use his weight to his advantage. The top man has most of the responsibility for keeping the cut straight on course and must pull the saw back up with his arms and shoulders alone.

The Pit

Full sawpits are over six feet deep and should be about four feet wide, lined on the sides with slabs or brick. The length of the pit is determined by the type of work being done—a house carpenter would use a longer pit than a wheelwright. Not only shops but also some of the larger estates had sawpits. Thomas Jefferson had one at Monticello. In *The Merry Wives of Windsor* six children disguised as hobgoblins scare Falstaff when they "from forth a sawpit rush at once." Traces of old sawpits are hard to find now, though. An archaeologist told me why this is. Apparently, when the change was made to power sawing and the old pits were no longer needed, they were cut up into small pieces and sold by the foot as post-holes.

Our sawpit is what might be called a half-pit. It is but 4½ feet deep; the rest of the necessary height is made up by the two post-mounted sills that run along its 16-foot length. The log being sawn is supported by two octagonal rollers whose bearing ends ride in strategically placed hollows in the tops of the long sills. The rollers are bored through on their ends to permit the insertion of a lever bar for rolling the log forward or back on the sills.

Many sawyers do not use a pit at all but rely on trestles and props to lift the log 8 feet in the air. It doesn't take too many days of this to convince you that it's easier to start digging.

Preparing the Log

At one time, few oak logs reached the sawpit with the bark still on. Vast quantities of oak and chestnut bark were consumed by the leather-tanning industry, and the bark was quite valu-

Trestles, sawn stock, and slab.

able. Since it was exceedingly difficult to debark a tree except in the spring when the sap was rising, most oak was felled and stripped at that time. This was contrary to the traditional preference of the woodworker, who claimed to want only the sap-down, winter-cut logs. In any case, it gave the buyer a good argument to use in haggling over the price of the log. Other barks were valuable as dyestuffs. Today, getting rid of the bark helps preserve the log from insects and decay and gives a better surface for marking the guidelines for sawing.

Depending on the size and quality of the material and the final product desired, a log may be sawn "in the round" or hewn flat on two or four sides. Flattening the sides with an axe rather than with the saw saves labor: the two processes proceed at about the same rate, but the axe occupies only one man, the saw, two. Prime timber for cabinet work or flooring or logs to be quarter sawn should be left in the full round so as not to waste any part. Logs to be sawn into boards of a constant width, such as siding, are hewn on two sides to a thickness equal to the width required. A log that is to go for structural timbers, however, is best handled by hewing all four sides to the appropriate multiple of the final dimensions, say, 8 by 9 inches to yield six 3-by-4-inch studs.

For hewing, and for sawing as well, the timber works much easier while it is still fresh and green. Once it is cut into the smaller dimensions, the wood will of course dry much faster than it would have in the whole log. Pine logs dry rapidly and are best worked within a few weeks of felling. White oak, elm, and walnut logs are not going to be much drier even a year after felling. They can sit in the yard until you get around to them; just don't let the elm go rotten.

Fresher wood does cut easier, but

dry timber will have done most of its shrinking and will retain the dimensions to which it is cut. The difference in ease of cutting is not all that great. An 8-inch-thick, fresh-cut yellow pine can be easily sawn at more than a foot a minute. Dry pine cuts at just about the same rate. Ten-year-old ebony of the same thickness can be ripped at about a third that speed. You can allow for shrinkage in green wood by cutting oversized and prevent distortion by careful layout.

Lining Out

The tools and procedure for lining out logs for sawing are virtually the same as those for hewing, with the addition of a pair of dividers for pacing off equal planks. Usually the most direct procedure is first to snap the guidelines as needed on the bottom side of the log and then roll it over into place on the pit. Now, at each end of the log, "plumb up" with a weighted string from these lines on the bottom to find the points to commence and end the lines on top of the log and snap them out.

Beyond marking the basic dimensions, there are a number of other points to consider in lining out a log. The first is that if the log has any bow in it, it is best to see that the bow is in the vertical plane during sawing. Even if the external evidence of the bow is removed in hewing, it remains in the grain of the log. Boards that have the grain moving across their faces are better than those that have it moving in and out. Another consideration is to have the pith of the log either split by or parallel with the saw kerf. Again, the object is to produce straight-grained lumber with minimal checking and distortion problems. Finally, be sure to allow not only for the loss in the kerf (sawdust) but for shrinkage and any cupping that may

A pine log laid out for quarter sawing.

need to be planed out. The boards take some, the saw takes some, and the plane takes some.

We have never had much use for spike dogs, the giant iron staples used to keep the log steady. Some people use them all the time, but we rely instead on wooden wedges and

Garland Wood checks the plumb of the cut on an ebony log.

chocks to keep the log plumb and steady. This may have something to do with what the pitman prefers to be hit in the head with.

Sawing

Starting a two-man saw with one tooth to the inch on the end of a log can be difficult until you get the knack of it. You want to hook one tooth about an eigth of an inch in on the line and then make one sure downward stroke. Until the gullets of the teeth are buried in the kerf, sawdust will spray out to the sides. Once you've cut an inch into the log, though, the heavy sawdust falls directly down about 2 feet in front of the pitman. He may wear a hat while he works, but not for fear of sawdust.

When the saw is far enough into the log to allow it, a wedge is driven into the log to keep the saw from being pinched. As the kerf progresses, another wedge is driven in further along and the two leapfrogged down the length of the cut.

Steering a pit saw is quite a trick, but once the technique is mastered, good sawyers can turn out precision planking, accurate to within a sixteenth of an inch, with ease. Most of the control is in the hands of the top sawyer, but both men must work together. The top handle is called the tiller—for good reason, as its length allows the exercise of precise and subtle control of the action of the saw. To stay on the top line, the top sawyer twists the tiller to point the teeth in the right direction.

The top man is in control of the bottom line as well. Responding to calls from the pitman, he throws the top of the saw to the same side as the indicated error while giving the tiller a slight twist to maintain position on the top line. Throwing the saw causes it to lever against the top edge of the

The open pit saw can cut curved stock like these shafts for the cartwright.

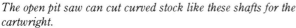

By throwing the saw to one side, the top man causes the bottom of the saw to move in the opposite direction. He keeps on the bottom line by throwing in the direction of the error.

kerf and the bottom to be forced in the opposite direction and back on the line down below. The pitman can steer to some extent with his handle, called the box, but the leverage from above is essential. Remember that all the steering in the world can be defeated by a cut that has fallen out of plumb.

Just as with the two-man crosscut saw, the work is done on the pull stroke. To try and push would kink the saw; there is some pushing, but it must be the lesser force. The pitman can ease the top sawyer's labor by bearing off the face of the kerf during the upstroke with a gentle lift to the rise of the box. Any drag caused by resting his arms on the upstroke will

wear out the sturdiest top man in about a minute. The top man can help his partner as well by the precise application of enough downward force to help the cut along but never so much as to cause the saw to chatter and jump.

And so it goes, sawing and wedging open the kerf until the pitman calls out to warn the top sawyer that they are about to cut into the support roller. As with any production job, the work is undertaken systematically. If the log is to receive more than one kerf, meaning cut into more than two pieces, all these kerfs will be sawn up to the first roller before continuing any one kerf to the end of the log.

Only after all of these cuts are

completed is the roller moved forward or the log slid back, the bottom handle or "box" of the saw removed by knocking loose its wedge, the saw reinserted in the kerf on the back side of the roller, and the box reattached. This move is where sawyers show some panache. The top sawyer draws the blade from the kerf like a sabre from a scabbard, walks with it along the log, and stabs it precisely through the next kerf. Beneath the log the pitman holds the box poised to capture the end of the blade the instant it appears. The pitman drives the wedge in the box tight, and the sawing continues.

Each kerf is cut to within inches of the end of the log and then stopped.

Sawyers have developed a reputation for a kind of elbow bending that is totally unrelated to that necessary for propelling the saw. To place their propensity for drink in perspective, I reprint here a table extracted from *London Labour and the London Poor* by Henry Mayhew in 1861. Note that sawyers rank thirty-fourth out of the sixty-six trades listed here.

COMPARATIVE TABLE OF DRUNKENNESS OF THE DIFFERENT TRADES IN LONDON.

Above the Average.

Button-makers, one individual in every	7·2
Tool-makers	10·1
Surveyors	11·9
Paper-makers and Stainers	12·1
Brass-founders	12·4
Gold-beaters	14·5
Millers	16·8
French Polishers	17·3
Cutlers	18·2
Corkcutters	19·7
Musicians	22·0
Opticians	22·3
Bricklayers	22·6
Labourers	22·8
General and Marine-store Dealers	23·2
Brushmakers	24·4
Fishmongers	28·2
Coach and Cabmen	28·7
Glovers	29·4
Smiths	29·5
Sweeps	32·2
Hairdressers	42·3
Tailors	43·7
Tinkers and Tinmen	45·7
Saddlers	49·3
Masons	49·6
Glassmakers, &c.	50·5
Curriers	50·6
Printers	52·4
Hatters and Trimmers	53·1
Carpenters	53·8
Ironmongers	56·0
Dyers	56·7
Sawyers	58·4
Turners	59·3
Engineers	59·7
Butchers	63·7
Laundresses	63·8

Painters	66·1
Brokers	67·7
Medical Men	68·0
Brewers	70·2
Clerks	73·4
Shopkeepers	77·1
Shoemakers	78·0
Coachmakers	78·8
Milliners, 1 in every	81·4
Bakers	82·0
Pawnbrokers	84·7
Gardeners	97·6
Weavers	99·3
Drapers	102·3
Tobacconists	103·4
Jewellers	104·5
Artists	106·3
Publicans	108·0
Average	113·8

Below the Average.

Carvers and Gilders	125·2
Artificial Flower Makers	128·1
Bookbinders	148·6
Greengrocers	157·4
Watchmakers	204·2
Grocers	226·6
Clockmakers	286·0
Parish officers	373·0
Clergymen	417·0
Servants	585·7

The above calculations have been made from the Official Returns of the Metropolitan Police. The causes of the different degrees of intemperance here exhibited, I leave to others to discover.

Changing kerfs.

In virtually every case all the boards are left connected at the back end and are broken apart only when the whole log is completed. The reason for this is obvious, for if one board were taken off at a time, the top sawyer would soon be trying to balance on the last two or three boards standing edge-wise. It wouldn't work.

Feather-Edged Weatherboards

One of the sawing jobs we get in our yard is weatherboard siding for houses. This type of horizontal siding is tapered from the bottom up so that the overlaps will lie flat. We cut them from clear yellow pine or tulip poplar by first hewing the log to 7½ inches thick. We then saw the log into inch-thick boards up to the first roller. Tilting the log with wedges so that the diagonals of the one-inch planks

Sawing feather-edged weatherboards.

Frame Saws

Until the eighteenth century most pit saws were narrow bands of steel stretched on wooden frames. This design was a function of the limitations of the technology of the time. Until the saw makers were able to roll out the broad expanse of steel required to make the unframed, or open, pit saw it was necessary for sawyers to fool with the somewhat cumbersome wooden frame. The frame pit saw does have the advantage that its narrow blade is able to turn the tight curves on the work found in shipyards and coach builder's and wheelwright's shops.

The history of pit sawing is intricately tied to the nature of the economy. In England to the end of the eighteenth century, the powerful and wealthy organized sawyers would regularly burn newly constructed sawmills to the ground. The sawyers pushed legislation by Parliament to ban the construction of horse-, wind-, or water-powered sawmills. The object was of course to protect their jobs. Here in the colonies, there was anything but a surplus of labor, and there were, of course, a lot of trees to cut. Water-powered sawmills were established almost immediately after settlement.

Pit sawing held on in the South, however, for a while longer. The wide coastal plain of the South made watermill construction more troublesome than it was in the North, where there was more fall on the rivers. And in the primarily agricultural and slave-holding South much capital was tied up in owning labor. With little money or thought left for investment in industry, pit sawing continued to be the way.

are plumb, we proceed to resaw each board in half on the diagonal. These cuts are not lined out with the snap line, but are done by both the top man and the pitman keeping $1/16$ inch from the kerf previously sawn. Cut in this manner, a single log can be stretched to cover one entire side of a house. Once the diagonal cuts are all done, we move the roller forward and continue the process down the log. We keep the log bound together with rope as the sawing progresses. Even a large log can start to get uncertain for the man standing on top of it when it's cut into two dozen slices along its length.

You can tell pit-sawn stock by the changes in the angles of the saw marks.

The frame pit saw.

The Governor's Walnut

Down in the creek bottom behind the old royal governor's house lived a right sizable walnut tree. Last winter the creek flooded long enough to smother its roots, and the tree died. I'm always interested in walnut trees for my own work, but this one looked big enough to be of interest to others besides myself.

I made inquiries with our gunsmith and cabinetmakers to see if they were in the market for good gunstock blanks and figured plank. The "flame"-figure walnut would come out of the upper length of the trunk from which the major branches forked out. The gunstock blanks, though, would start down in the root swell below ground level and run up about six feet.

This meant that the tree could not be cut down in the normal way. We would have to dig down around the tree, chopping roots as we went, to get the root swell for the gunstocks. In addition, once the tree was down, the division, the crosscut between the part for the gunsmiths and the part for the cabinetmakers, would come smack in the middle of the clear length of the log, not a comfortable cut to make for one who is usually intent on getting the longest clear length possible.

The tree had to fall in the right direction in order to land on flat ground where it would not be damaged. Fortunately, the tree already had a slight lean to that side. To encourage this tendency I climbed up and cut off the larger branches on the opposing side. To be safe, I also tied

Sharpening Pit Saws

The rip teeth on a pit saw are basically one hundred $\frac{1}{16}$-inch-wide chisels and must be sharpened as such. Mount the saw on a bench with the teeth upright at about elbow height. Joint the teeth (bring all to the same height) by drawing a six-inch file down the length of the saw until the tips of all the teeth are brightened. The file must be held at precisely 90 degrees to the side of the blade.

Use a round file to cut all the gullets to a depth of $\frac{3}{4}$ of an inch. The gullets need to undercut the face side of the teeth enough to give them a moderate hook.

Set the teeth by alternately bending them to opposite sides of the saw. You can use a slotted piece of iron as a wrest to bend each tooth one-third of its thickness to the side. The wrest may have a stop to gauge this setting, or you can sight down on the tooth from above and do it by eye.

Sharpen the face of each tooth square and flat across and then file

The top set of teeth are good for soft wood, the bottom set for hard.

the backs until the flats from the jointing disappear.

If the saw tends to pull to one side, it indicates either that an error has been made in one of these steps or that the log is out of plumb. Excessive hook in the teeth will cause the saw to chatter and jump; too little hook cuts too slowly. You need less hook and smaller teeth for very hard woods, more hook and larger teeth for soft. Teeth sharpened as suggested above will do quite well in both, however. The saw may need a half-hour touch-up every day if it is in constant use. Every few years it will need a day-long re-gulleting.

---

in a rope connected to a block and tackle to pull it over when the time came.

We went to it with shovels and axes, chopping and digging our way down. The creek went right by us about eight feet away, and from our position about two feet lower than the level of the creek we had the strange sensation of looking up at the water flowing by. The sky had been clear when we began in the morning, but now in early afternoon the breeze was picking up and clouds were packing in. Our work was the subject of much comment from passers-by, who

generally felt obliged to tell us how much work this looked like and how they thought it might start raining before we were done. We dug and chopped in shifts.

I had just climbed up out of the hole to sit on the berm and examine an interesting clump of rusty metal when another of the passing commentators stopped to watch. He stood for a second or so and informed us that the tree was leaning. Mark and Mike were still in the hole chopping roots, and I heard one of them call up in an irritated voice, "Yeah, we know, it's leaning the way we want it to go."

There was a pause from the fellow, and he said, "No, you don't understand, I mean that tree is leaning fast!"

I looked up to see that the top of the tree was surely headed over. The keystone root had been severed, but down at the base where we were working the movement was so slight that it could not be detected. "It's going you guys. Get out!" I yelled. They both scrambled from the hole. "Get your shovels. Get your shovels!" I shouted.

My concern for the shovels was perhaps inappropriate and in any case

Pit Saws, Tillers, and Boxes

I have worked with nine different pit saws in my time and can testify that they are highly individual items. Each saw has its own rhythm, determined by its weight, thickness, temper, tooth, and tiller. Most recently manufactured pit saws are not taper ground to be thinner on their back sides than they are on the tooth side. A new, untapered saw weighs half again as much as one of earlier manufacture and is also much harder to steer.

If you find an old saw and you're sure that it doesn't more properly belong in a museum collection, you can usually put the teeth in good cutting order, provided the steel is not excessively pitted. If the pitting has taken much away from the sides of the teeth, it will be difficult to put the saw right.

Many old saws will have lost several inches from years of sharpening. Since the middle of the saw is used the most, the line of the teeth will often appear concave from the side. This is no great problem; some saws have several tiller holes to allow the tiller to be set back to compensate for wear.

A good tiller should have a shaft about 2 feet long with the wooden handle about the same length. The shaft should sweep back about 3 inches toward the top sawyer. A tiller from the factory will have a single eye for the wedge bolt that attaches it to the saw. Many of the tillers made by local blacksmiths, however, fork and have two eyes to use two of the holes in the saw, the object being a firmer attachment. Local smiths appear to favor the "barrel eye" method of attaching the wooden handle to the shaft. Some factory tillers are made in this manner, but they are troublesome in that they are prone to wearing loose. The best tillers have their handles attached with an inset fork and twin tangs.

Boxes, the bottom handles, come in several forms, but all must be designed to be firmly attached yet easy to remove and refasten. The most common style combines iron and a foot-long wooden handle. Another variety is all wood, turned in the shape of a barrel with handles at either end. Both fit around the saw and are usually held with a wooden wedge. Other designs employ large wingnuts, but I have seen them only in pictures. Because the removable boxes are easily lost, few old saws that turn up still have them attached. For these the turned wooden type is the easiest to make.

The most frequent accidental injuries I have seen with pit saws occur when the box handle is not securely fastened and slips off on the downstroke of the pitman. This causes the pitman's face and the back of the blade to meet with some violence. Always double-check the box before you begin.

The tiller on the left came from the factory, the one on the right from a local smith.

Two boxes, the pitman's pride.

The blanks and a finished stock.

Digging it down.

came about three seconds too late. I saw them both turn to retrieve them and then hesitate in one of those exquisite moments of self-preservation and the jaws of the trap closed without them. The tree landed with a mighty *"thunk"* and wrenched the root mass from the hole, entwined with the mangled remains of the two shovels. Mark and Mike looked at the shovels and then they looked at me.

Once the logs were back at the saw pit, we worked them up into the gunstock blanks and cabinet planks. The job was stretched out over two weeks because we had a lot of other things to get done. The sawing went about like any big job, but I did notice one peculiar thing. Our sawpit is usually inhabited by several score of crickets, which hop about constantly, caroming off the walls. After a few days of sawing the dry walnut, however, the crickets were conspicuously absent. Whether the walnut dust did them in or they just left, I don't know, but if you ever want to get the crickets out of your sawpit . . .

THE HOUSEWRIGHTS

The Carpenter is employed in the Wooden-Work,
from the Foundation to the Top. . . . Strength is
the chief of his study.

R. Campbell, *The London Tradesman* (1747)

Bill Weldon laying up weatherboards.

In 1979 I left the business of making rakes and chairs and teaching workshops to join the community of craftsmen at Colonial Williamsburg as the master housewright. Although the restoration of the capital of the colony of Virginia to its eighteenth-century appearance had been in progress since the 1930s, the work had not before been undertaken with the original techniques. This was an entirely new position, and I was presented with the opportunity of building a program from the ground up.

Actually, though, we started below ground. Examination of the surviving original buildings showed that virtually all the material had been cut with pit saws. The first order of business, then, was establishing the sawpit and getting into the timber business.

There was, and is, so much to learn. The crew and I were essentially learning a new language in a forgotten dialect. What we knew to be right or best or easiest or strongest often had little relevance. We had to do it the way it was done or our work was meaningless.

A scientist answers questions by conducting experiments. To answer the question of how these people, our ancestors, worked and solved problems required the establishment of a grand experiment, the recreation of the working environment of eighteenth-century Tidewater Virginia builders.

I am well aware of how risky it is to draw historical conclusions from modern experience, but I am equally aware of how risky it is to work from written records alone. One can't recreate the music from the score unless he knows how to play the instruments. We work largely with original tools. We fell the timber within a mile of town and haul it back with teams of horses. Nails and hardware are all hand forged by our blacksmiths. Bricks are handmade. We make the

lime for mortar, plaster, and whitewash by burning oyster shell. We produce roofing tar from heart pine. Even the string for the chalk lines is hand-spun linen.

Artifacts to support the accuracy of the work range from the eighty-eight original buildings in the town to the archaeological collections of tools retrieved from excavations of wells and other sites throughout the area. The research libraries have the original builders' manuals from the period, as well as inventories and ledgers from Tidewater builders.

This record cannot be depended on entirely, however. Time has a way of skewing the evidence available from surviving artifacts. Buildings that are still about after several centuries are those that were built to last. The vast majority of buildings did not survive, and that includes a large proportion of the lower-class housing, which was probably of poorer construction. If we based our work on only the best buildings of a period, we would be misrepresenting that period. Survival may be an accident, but it selects for the fittest.

The same is true with tools. A tool may survive either because it was exceptionally well made or for the opposite reason. I have examined numerous axe heads that were found by archaeologists excavating old wells. The date of their burial can be determined fairly accurately by ceramics found in the same layer. This gives a random sample of the axe heads of the period perhaps, but I often wonder whether these axe heads represent only those that were being lost down wells. Are we looking only at the tools of the clumsy?

Nevertheless, it is the artifacts, the buildings in particular, that must speak. The marks of the tools left on the timbers record every stroke of the workman's arm, and that is what we are after: to preserve the process

as much as the product of that labor.

A kind of no-win situation arises when a small crew (at most we have six) attempts to recreate the work of eighteenth-century builders. If we were to work with boards and timbers that had been dimensioned by means other than pit sawing or hewing, we would throw the validity of the rest of our work into question. But if the same few men did all the falling, hauling, sawing, hewing, riving, carpentry, and joinery, we would again create an inaccurate situation. These were, as they are today, specialized trades, particularly in a town like Williamsburg.

The better of these choices, though, is certainly the latter. The ability to recreate the external form of colonial American buildings is widespread and well developed. It is the texture and context of the work that has been lost, and that is what we seek to recover.

Our work begins, as it always has, back in the woods. We fell the timber about a mile south of town, an easy hauling distance for the horses. We cut more pine than anything else. The longleaf pine that once grew here is no more, so we are forced to use loblolly instead. There is quite a difference in the old-growth longleaf and the loblolly in strength and durability, but it is about as close as we are able to come. Tulip poplar is the second most used tree, and it too has changed from what it used to be. The huge first-growth trees had a dark green heartwood that turned brown in the light and air. This old poplar could stand up to the elements as well as any wood, but it too is no more. White oaks are the other trees we fell. They are used almost exclusively for sill timbers, where their ability to resist decay can be used to advantage.

Once we're back at the work yard in town, we strip the oaks of their

Mark Berninghausen felling timber.

Chop in notches and split off the chunks in between.

Finish up with a broad axe.

bark. There used to be a tannery about a quarter mile from our yard, so we strip and stack the bark for sale as it would have been. Because at most only a few hours have elapsed between the felling of the tree and its arrival in town, it is easy to remove.

The white oak can sit in the yard many weeks before it starts to dry out or decay, but the pine and poplar must be seen to right away. Within a day or so the logs are laid out and hewn to their appointed dimensions. We hew beams by notching in every foot or so and then breaking off the chunks in between the notches. This same pattern of working can be seen quite clearly in the floor joists of a house that stands not half a block from our yard. Although it appears to have been built about fifty years after the time in which we're working, it follows the practice and pattern of the earlier structures in town. The notches were evenly spaced except where a knot in the log made it necessary to chop in directly on top of it. Unless a notch were chopped right

where this knot was, it would effectively peg the wood around it to the log, making it difficult to pop the chunk off with the axe.

The timbers we cut are pretty standard dimensions. A small out-building might have 6-by-8-inch sills, 4-by-6 posts, braces, plates, and joists, and 3-by-4 studs and rafters. A dwelling house needs larger sills, posts, braces, plates, and joists, but the studs remain a basic 3 by 4 inches. A builder in colonial Williamsburg would at times have been purchasing many of his building materials, rather than prepare them himself, and having standard sizes was the only way to do this.

As I said earlier, though, we cut everything ourselves and stockpile it for each building. Door and window stock and flooring go first and are stacked in the loft to dry. Sills and heavy beams come next, followed by the lighter stock, stuch as studs and weatherboards.

The framing timbers are cut before the studs and siding because they are

heavier and take longer to dry. They are never completely dry before we begin framing, for this could take many years. There are ways to compensate for shrinkage, though, and the timbers in existing buildings show that many were still relatively unseasoned when they were put in place. By cutting our mortices deeper than they need to be, for example, we lessen the chance that they will ride up on the tenons as the timbers dry.

The majority of the framing is done right in the yard, first the floor and then one wall at a time. When we complete an assembly, we disassemble it and stack it aside until we have completed the whole house frame. Working this way, two carpenters can frame an entire house. The big crew is hired only for the one or two days needed for assembly. House frames built in Virginia were shipped as far as Barbados.

We first cut the sills to length and prepare the corner joints. The long-wall sills are either morticed to receive the tenons on the sills of the

Morticing.

Each joint is numbered.

The stud nailed to the foot of the brace.

short wall or cut away on the underside to half lap on top of them. Next the corners on the short sills are prepared. The sills are then joined on their corners and the assembly brought square.

All measurement is done with the proverbial "ten-foot pole" and two-foot rules. We test for squareness in small angles by using wooden squares and in large angles by measuring out 3 units on one leg of the angle, 4 units on the other. When the length of the hypotenuse of this triangle is 5 units, the corner is at 90 degrees. As a final check we measure the diagonals of the rectangular frame. If the lengths of the two diagonals are equal, the corners are square.

Floor joists are either set into open-topped mortices in the sills or framed into their inner faces. Mortices in our house framing range between one and two inches wide and as long as can be managed without weakening either member. The rule of thumb in joining equal-sized timbers is to make the mortice and tenon

more than a third but less than a half of the width of the timbers. This rule appears to have been generally followed by the builders in our town. Examining the bottoms of mortices in existing buildings, I found that the bulk of the wood was only occasionally removed with a shell or "nose" auger before the remainder was squared up with a framing chisel. I have seen nothing that would suggest that corner chisels were used by carpenters at this time in this town. Remember that the twisted spiral auger with the pointed lead screw did not become common until about 1810. The nose auger works reasonably well, but it is a bit awkward to use; many mortices were cut with the framing chisel alone.

When all floor members are in place, we number them with Roman numerals to identify how the pieces are to go back together. Then we disassemble the frame and stack the floor joists aside. (If you have ever wondered why you use Roman numerals, just try and cut a regular

number 8 with a framing chisel.)

Next, the top of one sill is morticed to take the tenons on the bottom of the corner and intermediate posts. The rectangular posts are always set in with their wider face on the long wall of the building. Later buildings, built after 1780, may have posts that are hewn to an L-shaped cross-section, 4 or 6 inches thick on each arm of the L, so that the inside corner does not protrude into the room. The top plate is laid out simultaneously with the sill and morticed to take the tenons on the tops of the posts.

Braces are run from the sills to the corner posts and, in walls over 30 feet or so, to the intermediate posts as well. When we set in a brace, we almost always locate it exactly to coincide with the foot of a stud which will be nailed (yes, nailed) onto the upper side of the brace. The strength of these braces is in their resistance to compression: that is, they prevent the angles of the corners from becoming more acute under the pressure of wind loads. If the mortices in the sill

Setting in the braces.

for the braces closely abutted a mortice cut for another framing member, there would be a risk of shear failure and a consequent loss of brace strength.

The position of the foot of a brace, then, is determined by the spacing of the studs. Studs in Williamsburg houses are spaced on centers ranging from 18 to 28 inches in different buildings. (In smokehouses they may be only 6 inches apart to prevent a thief from tearing off siding and squeezing through. When a considerable portion of your income is tied up in smoked hams, you build a smokehouse like a safe.)

The location of the mortice in the post determines the slope of the brace. The brace mortice in the post may be cut in at any convenient height as long as it is about two-thirds up the post. Since the braces are not at a convenient slope to be laid out mathematically, the usual practice is to cut the mortices in the sill and the post, assemble the wall on the ground, lay the brace on the side where it is to go, and scribe its length and the angles of its tenon shoulders. I always feel sort of dumb when I do this because it is essentially trial-and-error fitting. This is the way it was done though. It's the "stick-it-there-and-if-there's-a-knot-move-it" school of building.

Once we have framed, numbered, and stacked away the walls and floor system, we set out the plates on the ground and cut in the ceiling joists. Often, rather than use an elaborate multistepped lap which would retain the maximum strength of both members, we simply cut away the top of the plate and the underside of the joist in a simple interlock, as was done in many of the buildings of this period. Only the end joists require pegging.

Generally, we use marking gauges to determine the depth of this cut, always gauging down from the upper face of the joists. This throws any error to the underside of the joists, leaving the top relatively level. The top of the joists will be covered with floorboards, which is carpenter's

Trimming the joists.

The timbers go down to the site.

work. The underside will receive the laths to hold the plaster ceiling. It's easier to cover irregularities with plaster than with floorboards, and since this is not something that the carpenters will have to worry about, that is where the error goes.

By the time the main frame is ready, the masons will have completed the foundation, and we can move the timbers down to the site, raise the main frame, and begin the roof framing.

In virtually every dwelling in town, the joists are made to extend out over the top plate to form the base for the classic boxed cornice. On top of the ends of the joists is set what is called a "false plate." This false plate is the seat for the ends of the rafters and may be of two types. The simplest and most common is the board false plate, a 1 by 8 nailed to the top end of the joist extension. The ends of the rafters are attached by nailing down through them into this board.

A rarer and more interesting version is the tilted false plate. A rectangular timber is cut diagonally away on its underside so that its outer face matches the slope of the rafters. The rafters are cut away on their undersides to seat on the inner slope and lie flat on the outer. Pegs through the outer side hold everything firmly. The inner seat in the rafter is made by sawing halfway through at right angles to the length of the rafter. The surface that sits flush on the outer face of the false plate is then cut in with a carpenter's adze. The scalloped way in which this cut is formed has been accepted as a decorative motif in buildings that have no need of such a joint.

The steel square so commonly used in roof framing today was less common in the eighteenth century. Instead of pacing off the "rise over run" with the square to determine the length and angles of the rafters, we use a formula based on a set propor-

Pole rafters on a board false plate. · *A tilted false plate.*

tion of the length of the attic floor joists. If we want a roof with a pitch of 45 degrees, for example, we pace off the length of the joists with a pair of dividers, setting and resetting until we hit on exactly 24 moves from one end to the other. We then use this setting on the dividers to pace off 17 of these moves on the rafter stock to determine the precise rafter length that will give us a roof pitch of 45 degrees. In other words, if a joist is 24 steps from front to back, two rafters of 17 steps each will form a peak angle of 90 degrees when set on top of it. Other proportional pitches of rafter length over joist span used at this time are: $3/4$, $5/6$, $4/5$, $7/9$, $2/3$, $5/8$, $3/5$, $7/12$, $4/7$, and $5/9$.

After determining the length of the rafters and the spread of their base, we lay a rafter pair out on the ground at the angle at which they will be set. We then scribe the angle of their crossing at the ridge and the proper seating angles on the false plate at their base. The top is then joined with either a half-lap or bridle joint, nailed or pegged, the feet cut to the appropriate seat, and a wind beam nailed or pegged across the pair about a third of the way down from the peak. Subsequent pairs are made the same way and stacked until all are done. We then hoist them up on top of the frame and set them all in place, securing them with a long length of scrap wood nailed to their undersides as a

temporary brace. No ridge pole is used. The roof is now ready for covering.

This completes the main frame of posts, beams, and rafters. Before we can side the building, however, the studs must go in. These are sometimes cut into the frame only after the main frame has been joined. They do not form any real part of the structural support, but serve mainly as something to nail the siding to on the outside and the plaster lath to on the inside. The feet of these studs are usually held at the bottom by mortice and tenon joints, but often their tops are joined to the plate by a peculiar "miter lap." First, two kerfs are sawn into the diagonal of one edge of the

Trim the rafter feet with a carpenter's adze.   *Rafters, collars, and shingle lath in place.*

Setting in gable-end pole studs.

overhead beam and the wood in between chiseled out. The top of the stud is then cut away in the corresponding angle to fit into this pocket. To assemble, the stud is put into place at its base and then pushed into the slot at the top. The top joint is then secured with a nail or two. The advantage of this system is that it minimizes the amount of precise fitting. It's necessary only to get the outside dimensions of a wall true and square then fill in with studs quickly cut to fit at their given locations.

Trim and Siding

The concept of forming an outline and then coming back and filling up in between is carried on in other aspects of the building as well. The first finish work done on the outside is the setting in of the door and window trim and corner boards. The latter define the sharp angles of the structure and are thus exposed to a great deal of wear. For this reason, they are commonly finished on their exposed edge with a corner bead. In effect, this

Miter-lapped studs.

The beaded corner board and T-head nail.

"beading" moves the sharp square edge back away from the most exposed position and leaves in its place a rounded profile. The edge is still sharply defined to the eye and will remain so over centuries of wear.

We nail all trim boards on with the equivalent of flush-set finishing nails. The regular "rose heads" of these wrought nails are hammered flat to form a narrow T-head. We often do these ourselves by cold hammering on an old anvil. The T-head is driven in with the grain of the wood, flush with the surface.

After we have the trim boards in place, we fill in the space between them with weatherboarding. These weatherboards are either taper-sawn "feather edged," each one overlapping the one below it, or flush-set planking with rabbets cut into their upper and lower edges to form a shiplap.

On both types of weatherboarding, the procedure for fitting them tight within the trim boards is the same. We first saw one end off square and butt it up to the trim board. On the other end we place a U-shaped guide called a "preacher" around the weatherboard and flush up against the edge of the trim board. The outer face of the preacher is exactly in line with the inner face, which abuts the corner board. By scratching a line down the outer face, we have a precise indication of where to cut the weatherboard to get a good fit.

All weatherboarding is laid in sequence from the bottom up. Shiplapped boards are often random widths but are planed parallel, so once we have the bottom course on right, we can set each sucessive course tight on top of the course below and the wall moves upward maintaining the horizontal orientation of the first bottom board. Feather-edged boarding does not have a set overlap. Each course must be gauged upward from the bottom edge of the one below it. We always try to get the lower edge of tapered weatherboards that are interrupted by a window to hit right on the bottom edge of the window sill. Thus, the amount of exposure of these boards is often determined by pacing off the distance from the lower edge of the window sill to the bottom of the first weatherboard with a pair of dividers. When we hit on an agreeable exposure that will make the boards correspond, we use

Scribe the weatherboards to a tight fit with the aid of the "preacher."   *A new boxed cornice.*

this exposure all around the building.

The next bit of finishing work is boxing in the cornice around the extended attic joists. First on are the facia and soffit boards. We nail the vertical facia into the end grain of the joists and the horizontal soffit board to the undersides of the joists. The facia hangs slightly below the soffit, forming a drip edge to keep water from running into the cornice and rotting it out.

The bed moulding is nailed into the angle between the top weatherboard and the soffit; the crown moulding, into the angle between the facia and the shingle overhang. It looks good and keeps the bats out of the attic.

On the gable ends, we cap the end of the cornice with a board called a cornice stop. This cornice stop is made the same thickness as the corner boards and the siding so that it can be covered in turn by the rake boards that cover the gap between the gable end siding and the slope of the roof. This rake board, which is made to be slightly wider at its base than it is at the top, finishes the gable end of the house quite nicely.

Flooring is also carpenter's work. More often than not, the floorboards are inch-thick heart yellow pine, quarter-sawn, tongue and groove or splined boards laid directly on the floor joists. These floorboards were the first boards cut for the house, so they should be well seasoned by the time we are ready to lay them.

To prepare a rough-sawn floorboard for laying, we first plane it true and straight on one edge, scribe a line for the other edge parallel to the first, and bring that edge true. We then plane the best face flat and true and plow the groove and plane the tongue. After the tongue and groove are planed, we run a gauge set to the thickness of the thinnest board down both edges, gauging always from the face side of the floorboard. Rather than plane all the undersides level, though, we simply run a rabbet plane down both edges of the underside of each board until we reach the gauged lines. When we lay the floor, we adze out down to the level of these rabbets just the portions that ride on the joists, allowing all the upper faces to lie at the same height.

Before laying the floor, we inspect the joists with levels and by eye to see that all are in the same plane.

The rake boards go up on a hen house.

Floor boards are adzed to a common thickness only where they cross a joist.

High spots are adzed down and low spots furred up. The first board is nailed down right against the wall with the same sort of flush-set nails used on the trim work. Adjoining boards are adzed out where they cross the joists and fitted up in turn but not nailed down as of yet. When we have a few feet of flooring set down and level, we bore a 1-inch-diameter hole into every other joist about an inch beyond the edge of the last board. We set iron pins into these holes. Then, using wooden wedges driven between the pins and the last board, we tighten up the set of boards until they scream and then nail them down. After removing the wedges and iron pins, we go on to the next set. The sight of these peg holes left in the

tops of the joists of buildings whose floors have been removed has mystified many a restorer.

Once the floors are in, the joiners go to work installing windows, doors, staircases, and interior trim. In our way of working, the trim goes up first and the plaster is laid up to it. The plaster is set on strips of pine lath that are nailed closely together to cover all walls and ceilings. This really belies the popular notion that they didn't have nails back then. The frame of the house is secured with pegged joints, but only because this is a much stronger way of building. There may be more nails in one room of an eighteenth-century house than in an entire modern house.

We make plaster and whitewash

from lime burned from oyster shell. There is no limestone in our region, but shells are the same thing; they just have not been pressured into rock.

Shells are calcium carbonate. When they are heated in a small kiln, the carbon dioxide is driven off, leaving calcium oxide. The shells retain their shape, but have now turned yellowish. They are now quicklime shells. We shovel these shells out of the kiln once it and the shells have cooled, set them in a vat or a pit dug in the sand, throw water on them, and stand back. For about five minutes nothing happens. Then a bit of steam begins to rise from the mass. In ten minutes the reaction is going strong, making what looks like a volcano of boiling

Lew LeCompte at the lime kiln.

chalk. The water is taking the place of the carbon dioxide and the reaction releases a tremendous amount of heat.

Joseph Moxon described it best in the seventeenth century. "And the Fire in Lime burnt, Asswages not, but lies hid, so that it appears to be cold, but Water excites it again, whereby it Slacks and crumbles into fine Powder." After twenty minutes the pile of wet shells has become an overflowing mound of pure white powder, hydrated lime or calcium hydroxide. Mixed with more water, horsehair, and sand, it forms plaster. Without the horsehair it makes mortar for the brick work. A bit of salt added to the mixture gives whitewash for the outside.

Shells, clay, water, wood, and iron—a home.

This is a beginning. Slowly we learn to assimilate the work, as one who studies ancient languages finds himself thinking in ancient Greek. The meaning slowly becomes clearer, as we discover more of the lost vernacular forms of building. Rural patterns

that have left only the faintest traces must be painstakingly pieced together like bits of broken pottery. A few postholes here, a tantalizing paragraph there. Many of the pieces are missing, and much must be left to educated guesswork. Building a house this way takes the cooperation of many different trade specialties: woodsmen, sawyers, smiths, carpenters, masons, plasterers, and joiners. Our work also requires the additional trades of the historian, the archaeologist, and the curator and,

most important, the support of people from all over the world who share with us the desire to learn from our common past. Each beam is raised with the help of a thousand invisible hands. It's a deep, good feeling when the house goes up.

Selected Chronological Bibliography

Moxon, Joseph. *Mechanick Exercises*. London, 1683.

Lawson, John. *A New Voyage to Carolina*. London, 1708.

Neve, Richard. *The City and County Purchaser and Builder's Dictionary*. London, 1726.

Diderot, Denis. *Encyclopédie*. Paris, 1765.

Roubo, A. *L'Art du Menuisier*. Paris, 1769.

Parker, Thomas N. *Practical Inquiry Concerning . . . Gates and Wickets*. London, 1801.

Nicholson, Peter. *The Mechanic's Companion*. Philadelphia, 1859.

Griswold, Lean S. "The Novaculites of Arkansas." Annual Report of State Geologist, Arkansas, 1891.

Kimball, Fiske. *Domestic Architecture of the American Colonies and of the Early Republic*. New York: Scribner, 1922.

Graham, Frank D. *Carpenter's and Builder's Guide (1st edition)*. Theo. Audel, 1923.

Sturt, George. *The Wheelwright's Shop*. Cambridge: Cambridge University Press, 1923.

Kelly, J. Fredrick. *Early Domestic Architecture of Connecticut*. New Haven: Yale University Press, 1929.

Mercer, Henry C. *Ancient Carpenter's Tools*. Bucks County Historical Society, 1929.

Talbot, Antony, ed. *Handbook of Doormaking, Windowmaking, and Staircasing*. 1920(?).

Rose, Walter. *The Village Carpenter*. Cambridge: Cambridge University Press, 1938.

Green, Charlotte H. *Trees of the South*. Chapel Hill: University of North Carolina Press, 1939.

Hartley, Dorothy. *Made in England*. London: Methuen, 1939.

Shurtleff, H. R. *The Log Cabin Myth*. Cambridge: Harvard University Press, 1939.

Edlin, H. L. *Woodland Crafts in Britain*. B. T. Batsford, 1949.

Harlow and Harrar. *Textbook of Dendrology*. New York: McGraw-Hill, 1964.

Whiffen, Marcus. *The Eighteenth Century Houses of Williamsburg*. Williamsburg: Colonial Williamsburg, 1960.

Goodman, W. L. *The History of Woodworking Tools*. New York: McKay, 1964.

Panshin and deZeeuw. *Textbook of Wood Technology*. New York: McGraw-Hill, 1964.

Hummel, Charles F. *With Hammer in Hand*. Charlottesville: University Press of Virginia, 1968.

Hindle, Brooke, ed. *America's Wooden Age: Aspects of It's Early Technology*. Tarrytown: Sleepy Hollow Restorations, 1975.

Salaman, R. A. *Dictionary of Tools*. New York: Scribner, 1975.

Buchanan, Paul. *Eighteenth-Century Frame Houses of Tidewater Virginia*. Monograph in *Building Early America*. Philadelphia: Chilton, 1976.

Kababian, P. B. *American Woodworking Tools*. Greenwich: New York Graphic Society, 1978.

Sellens, Alvin. *Woodworking Planes*. Alvin Sellens, 1978.

Cummings, Abbot Lowell. *Framed Houses of Massachusetts Bay, 1625–1725*. Cambridge: Harvard University Press, 1979.

Little, Elbert L. *Audubon Society Field Guide to North American Trees*. New York: Knopf, 1980.

Townsend, Raymond R. *The Petite Gazette*. Williamsburg.

Many of the books listed here are available through the book services provided by the Early American Industries Association, a nonprofit educational organization which also publishes the journal *The Chronicle*. For information write Mr. John S. Watson, Treasurer, EAIA, PO Box 2128, Empire State Plaza Station, Albany, N.Y. 12220.

Index